Dear Aunty Karen,

I hope you enjoy the S on page 165).

From Joss

Joss (signature)

P.S. Keep this safe when I'm a famous author it will be valuable.

Crazy Cab Stories
Volume 2

An Anthology of Young Authors.

Crazy Cab Stories Volume 2
ISBN: 978-1-913781-04-0

Published by CAAB Publishing Ltd (Reg no 12484492)

C.A.A.B
PUBLISHING

Foxbridge drive, Chichester, UK
www.caabpublishing.co.uk

All text copyright © of the Authors
Cover design copyright © CAAB Publishing Ltd
Additional photoshop elements from brusheezy.com

All rights reserved. No part of this book may be scanned, uploaded, reproduced, distributed, or transmitted in any form or by any means whatsoever without written permission from the author, except in the case of brief quotations embodied in critical articles and reviews.

This is a work of fiction. Names, characters, business, events and incidents are the products of the author's imagination. Any resemblance to actual persons, living or dead, or actual events is purely coincidental.

First Published 2020
Printed in the UK

British Library Cataloguing in Publication data available

With special thanks to the Judges:

F.J.Beerling – Author
Facebook.com/fairyfayeB

Alexandria Brown – Author
Gemmastersauthors.yolasite.com

Suzi White – Illustrator
Instagram.com/suziwhite123

For their help with picking a winning story.
It was a tough choice as the quality of the entries of extremely high.

Also, thank you to all those that sent in their hard work, not all were chosen but if your name appears in this book, you should be very proud indeed.

London Underground	Esme Bennett	5
The Time Travelling Taxi	Isobelle Lane	9
Lilly and the Magic Taxi	Brooke LoPinto	13
The Fairies' Taxi	Chloe Lennon	16
The Tale of Lightening and Infinity	Felix Russell	19
Imagination	Freya Crump	23
Escape	Jessica Thomas	26
The Magic Map	Siva Patel	29
The Rat's Revenge	Ibrahim Ali Azhar	33
Taxi Ride To Destiny	Amelie Lee	35
Ava, Monty and the Magic Taxi	Maya Walther	39
The M Taxi	Simon Saraf	43
The Taxi of The Huehounds	Arnav Kasireddy	45
Madison and the Magic Taxi Cab	Abbie Clarke	48
The Game	Suleman	52
Daisy's New Friend	Chloe Stevens	55
Ginger Taxi and Candy Rush	Autumn Gristy	59
The Power Stones	Maria	62
Chaos in Space	Matthew Jenkins	66
The Crazy Trip	Phoebe Golledge	70
The Mystery Of The Three Headed Creature	Adam Seymour	74
A Mystical Spell	Amisha K. Davies	78
Enchanted Talking Taxi	Alannah Batteux	82
Puddles and the Magic Taxi	Hannah Jones	86
Dystopia	Catherine Katesmark	89
The Haircut	Tilly O'Shea	93
The Magic Poster	Arthur Moynihan	97
The Coalfear Cab	Bella Holland	101
Temperature Rising	Hannah McCormack	106
Emily and Chloe's Amazing Magical Taxi Adventure Saving Mr Watson!	Louisa Kennedy	110
The Cashew Quest	Alistair Hsiao	114
Josh and the Magic Elves	Charlie Macfarlane	118
Video Game Travels	Struan Wallace	120
The Explorers Dream	Eliot Santell	123
The Flying Taxi	Selina Scally	127
The Three Miracles	Rachel Harwood	131
Evie	Emily Locke	134
Josh and the Magic Taxi	Daniel Gawish	137
The Craziest Day Ever!	Emily	140
In the City	Samuel Au	143
The Adventures of Intrepid Isidora	Isidora Holms	146
The Berry, The Breath and The Bark	Dylan Wade	149
The Powerful Portal	Silas Santell	153
The Cat Taxi Service	Selina Brown	157
The Taxi to Impossible Places	Olivia Bunimovich	161
Felicity	Joss Steel	165
Taxi Cab 54321	Verity Callaghan	168
The Video game Adventure	Ruairidh H	172
The Magical Keys	Isaac Manuell	176

Our Winning Entry
Featured in both Crazy Cab volumes

London Underground
by Esme Bennett aged 9

He stood outside his office, tapping his Rolex watch furiously with the rain running down the umbrella in his hand. He put on a fading grin as the taxi pulled up towards him. You may be wondering who 'He' is? He is the most powerful and rich business owner in our city, named John Ramien. He climbed into the taxi and the driver said in a quiet tone, "I'm so sorry I was late sir, it will not happen next time." John, being his normal rude self, replied, "I'm sorry, but there won't be a next time as you are twenty minutes late! Now get me across London to the Conference Centre. I have a very important meeting!"

As the taxi sped away, the driver made one more remark, "May I ask sir, why are you not wearing a mask? I could refuse to take you…"

"That's my business!" his passenger hissed. "Now, hurry up or I'll be speaking to your boss about your rudeness and your lateness."

The taxi raced along but John began to feel unwell. His head slumped against the misted windowpane and as he stared out, he thought the pedestrians looked rather ghostly with their mouths covered with masks because of the pandemic. What was wrong with him? He started going through the files in his briefcase. Then he noticed a small mask tucked in a side pocket, packed with his lunch by his wife that morning. He had refused to take it, "So silly," he had said to her, "so unnecessary."

Suddenly, John noticed that they were not on the road anymore but driving through a graveyard. "Stop this taxi or I will report you to the police," John stammered. He reached for his phone, but there was no signal.

"No need for that, sir. Just a short cut," the driver replied, as they disappeared below ground.

John was frozen in his seat. The car stopped in front of an iron door in the earth walls. He asked the driver, "Why are we here?"

The driver replied calmly, "Please step out of the car and open that door. I will wait for you here."

John felt compelled to do as the driver said and he found himself walking down a wide staircase. To his surprise a man in a uniform passed him, running up the other side with great urgency. "Watch your step, guv. Hope you've got your gas mask – Germans dropping all sorts tonight!" John was extremely puzzled. Was this a prank? He reached the bottom stair and as he turned the corner he was astounded at the sight. He was standing on a Tube platform covered in a sea of people.

The people were all different ages; chatting and eating, playing games, or sleeping. All of them were dressed in very old-fashioned clothing, some were wearing gas masks. A Blitz reenactment of some kind, John thought. He wondered whether it was an important anniversary today, but he decided it wasn't and that these people must be down here for some sort of silly dressing-up party.

John remarked at a thin man sat on the cold ground, "Why are you people down here, and what is that ridiculous thing on your face?" He pulled the mask off. It tumbled to the ground in what felt like slow motion. They were the longest seconds of John's life. John felt incredibly stupid as if the whole world was watching him. The thin man looked shocked and angry. John ran back around the corner and onto the opposite platform.

On this side were another group of people who also seemed to be sheltering. They looked tired and very sad. Their clothes and hairstyles were different from the people on the first platform. Some of the clothes looked very dirty and black. People were coughing, some had rags covering their mouths. A

6

funny burning smell was in the air. John listened to two women talking close by.

"How many did they get out of those houses?" One woman asked with a concerned look on her face.

"Not enough!" the second woman replied, "once that Zeppelin came down, it set the whole of Compton Road alight."

"Lucky to be down here, can't breathe up on the street," the first woman exclaimed.

John slowly realised he was in the London of the past and he must be a TIME TRAVELLER! He rushed back up the stairs but found the iron door closed. John banged and yelled. Eventually, the door gave way and there was the taxi on the other side.

John breathed heavily as he stepped back inside the car. The taxi driver asked him if he was ok. He responded, "No, you fool! I'm not. What kind of a question is that? Just get me out of here!" The taxi driver started the engine and they sped away once again.

John decided he would question the driver about what had happened in the tunnels. "The things I've seen tonight, I can't help feeling, I've been shown them for a reason…" he mumbled.

"You have," confirmed the driver.

"Why?" John enquired, dreading the answer.

"All will become clear. Just one more stop." They were heading deeper and deeper into the earth. After what seemed a very long time, the driver slowed the taxi and stopped the engine.

John got out of the car as he had done before, but this time, to his surprise, the driver got out with him. It was the first time John had seen him properly. The driver was tall. He had a young face, but he seemed worn-out as if he'd seen a lot of life.

"Look around you," the taxi driver said. John obeyed. "We are in the catacombs. These walls are home to all of the dead of London. Those who died when past diseases and misfortunes hit the city. These people often didn't know what killed them or how to protect themselves, they just ended up here. You know how to protect yourself and other people. Yet you choose not to. You're rude, selfish, and nasty. Perhaps, I should leave you down here?"

"Don't do that!" exclaimed John. "I'll… change. Please." John fell to his knees and scrabbled in his briefcase to grab his mask and put it on. He then shut his eyes tight and hugged himself with fear. What an afternoon it had been!

The next thing he felt was the sound of the taxi engine beneath him. They were back in the taxi and travelling upwards at great speed. Soon the streetlight burst through the windows and John could see they were above ground again. The taxi turned a corner and stopped abruptly. "This is your stop, sir," the taxi driver said, as if nothing had happened.

"How much do I owe you?" John whispered. The driver did not answer. John climbed out of the car in disbelief. As the taxi moved away, John could see the lights of the Conference Centre. Perhaps, he'd fallen asleep on the way and it was all a strange dream? As he walked up the steps, the phone rang in his pocket. He fumbled to answer it. "Hello – is that Mr Ramien?" said the voice on the other end of the line. "This is Capital Taxis. Our driver's waiting outside your place of work and I'm just phoning to see if you still need a ride to the Conference Centre this evening?"

The Time Travelling Taxi
by Isobelle Lane aged 11

Some people believe that the time travelling taxi cab is a myth, others believe it is real. Only those who have experienced it for themselves know if it's true…

One afternoon, the taxi cab pulled up to collect a lad named Jake. He was chosen only because of his bad actions and decisions. As Jake tumbled into the car, the driver never said a word.

Jake slumped in the car and it immediately sped off. Jake was flung back in to his seat and started being arrogant and obnoxious, shouting at the driver (who took no notice). With its tinted windows, no handles, and gadgets everywhere, Jake realised this wasn't an ordinary taxi cab! He became more and more agitated as he continued to shout at the driver who simply stared ahead with his steely eyes.

As the journey went on, Jake lost track of where he was, and the driver definitely didn't seem to be taking him home. Jake banged on the door and made as much noise as possible but still the driver never said a word.

"Let me out you crazy freak!" Jack screeched at the top of his lungs. There was no response.

After ten minutes of shouting from Jake, the driver pulled down a side street and into a deserted car park on the edge of London. He stopped the engine, turned his head and looked Jake straight in the eyes. Without a word spoken he pressed a button on the steering wheel and a massive screen dropped down from the ceiling. Three words appeared: 'Time to reflect'.

All of a sudden, the cab spun around and around, making Jake sick with dizziness. With an enormous bang, they stopped abruptly in front of his old school. Videos of Jake as a young boy flashed on to the screen inside the taxi cab. One by one they showed Jake behaving badly during his school life. Jake was shocked and angry.

"Who are you? A freaky stalker?! Why are you doing this?"
The driver, still without saying a word, pointed to the corner of the screen where the words, 'time to reflect' still showed menacingly, as if taunting Jake.

Videos of Jake doing cruel things to friends and family over the years played on for the next twenty minutes. Jake fidgeted uncomfortably in the back seat while staring at the screen.

"Ok, ok, I get it but why me? Why are you doing this to me? Where did you get all this?"

All of a sudden, the screen changed. Three words read 'Time to change' and the cab engine roared back to life and the cab darted forwards like the fastest rollercoaster Jake had ever been on. When it came to a stop, they arrived at a place Jake had not seen before with people on the streets and burnt-out buildings everywhere they looked.

The videos that then played on the screen were not familiar, but Jake soon realised what was happening. He was being shown what his future would end up like if he continued to act in the horrible way that he had been.

One video showed Jake in prison after being arrested. Jake became more and more anxious and terrified about his future. His stomach twisted with guilt as he started to understand what this was all about. Another video of an older Jake flashed up. He was in a dilapidated room with a few pieces of furniture, all alone and looking hungry. Jake had to turn away; it was overwhelming. His mind began to spin as all the memories of the horrible things he had ever done all came flooding back to him.

Just as Jake began to think he had done too much wrong in his life to ever come back from it and to turn it all around, another three words appeared on the screen as he looked up – 'Believe in yourself'.
Seconds later, the engine roared and the taxi cab slowly started reversing out into the street. After driving through empty roads for ten minutes, Jake started to recognise buildings and they drove past the place he had been picked up from earlier. He couldn't help but think about what he'd done in the past. Eventually, the driver pulled up outside Jake's house. Relieved that the door opened by itself, Jake looked at the driver who gave a reassuring nod but still never said a word. Jake slammed the door shut and the taxi cab drove off into the darkness.

Jake turned around and was surprised to see his parents waiting for him on the doorstep, they normally never cared where Jake went and what time he got back.

That night, Jake laid on his bed looking out the window at the stars. He knew that the next day he needed to start to change and make up for being the old him or else he could end up in prison! He decided that from that day onwards, he would be careful about every word that came from his mouth.

First thing in the morning, Jake went downstairs and made his parents' breakfast in bed. They were pleasantly surprised but mainly shocked. Jake said sorry for everything he had done in the past to all the people he had hurt by saying rude things and pulling stupid pranks that did nothing apart from make strangers laugh. Jake decided he wouldn't waste his life; he would study for his career and future.

Lilly and the Magic Taxi
by Brooke LoPinto aged 9

It was a usual Monday morning in London, a woman walked down the street with her daughter, a young girl named Lilly, with short brown hair, light hazel eyes, red shimmering shoes, and a long flower covered dress that she would twirl from time to time.

Lily's mother wore a long black waistcoat, she had long brown wavy hair, and short navy boots, and a small chained bag that dangled over her shoulder and swayed in the wind against the backdrop of the busy city.

The tall glass buildings overlooked the cars that speedily ran along the roads and the tall lampposts shone on the streets. As Lilly and her mother were strolling along the street, they came to a lovely posh shop. Inside the shop, they found all the clothes they needed for Lilly's school from shoes to skirts, from socks to shirts. However, just as Lilly was walking to the cashier to pay for the items she had collected, she noticed something strange outside the window. A black taxi cab popped out of the clouds and landed on the road. Lilly dropped the clothes on the floor and ran to see the taxi. It had a sign on it saying, 'Drive me'. As she ran, Lilly's money had fallen out of her dress pocket, but she was too excited to notice. Lilly grabbed the sign and sat it on the floor of the taxi. As she slid into the seat, she saw lots of different buttons. The buttons listed different destinations, different sizes, and different sections of the car. Without thinking about it, Lilly pressed a button saying, 'taxi kitchen' and with a rattle, Lilly's chair lifted off the ground and the floor moved bringing Lilly to the back of this giant taxi where she found a kitchen. There was a cupboard with pictures of food and just as Lilly watched the photos dance across the cupboard, she saw a macaroon appear. Her hand trembled, she wished to have the macaroon in her hand and before she knew it Lilly was holding a light, pink raspberry macaroon. On the other side of the room was the dinner table. It was one meter off the ground, with all the food, cutlery and drinks for any type of meal. Lilly tried and tried to fly up high to reach the table, but she could not reach it. Then, as Lilly tried for the third time to jump in the air, she flew to the top of the taxi and her feet dangled like a bright chandelier shining upon the room. Then she slowly floated to her seat and she was sitting on a dark red, velvet cushioned chair. Whilst sitting there she reached out for a dish of spaghetti and meatballs. When Lilly had finished her meal, the floors changed, and she got whisked away to the front of the taxi. "Where shall I go?", thought Lilly curiously. "Aha" she said, "I will go to Blackheath Village." Lilly pressed the small, glowing blue button and in a blink of an eye, she arrived at her destination. As Lilly got out of the taxi, she spotted a little ice cream shop called Madeleines. Lilly locked the taxi and wandered over to the shop. Inside she saw all different kinds of flavoured ice cream from caramel to cookie dough, to Oreo to Malteser. But of all the flavours she chose a cone of caramel ice cream. The cashier handed her the cone and waited for Lilly to pay. However, Lilly reached into her dress pocket and to her surprise, there was no money in her pocket. As Lilly turned around to hand her ice cream back to the cashier, she spotted a five-pound note under her foot. Lilly grabbed the note and sighed in relief as she gave the note to the cashier. Lilly devoured her delectable treat on the way to the taxi. When she had reached the place where she had parked, she noticed the taxi was gone, and there was only a rainbow mark with a note saying, 'Destination the Heath'. As Lilly picked up the note, she heard a loud crash of thunder and a bright yellow light that teleported her to a long grassy area where she saw boys and girls playing in the fresh air. In front of her she found her shiny black taxi. Lilly hopped inside and decided to take a rest, as she was very tired. But she found it hard to see the button into the bedroom. She then fell asleep on all the buttons and was suddenly travelling to a mystery destination somewhere in the world. When Lilly had awakened, she found herself in New York City. "Where am I?" exclaimed Lilly, as she removed her hands from the destination buttons where her head was resting. She stood up and opened the taxi door to find herself under the sun's warmth and being overlooked by the skyscrapers. Two feet away Lilly spotted a large pretzel stand called Doctor Salt, a worldwide pretzel company. Lilly then remembered that she did not have any change from the caramel ice cream she had in Blackheath Village. But Lilly had a cunning plan that was bound to work. As she patiently waited in the queue, she noticed she was following a rather large lady in line. "May I please have five large pretzels." said the woman in front of her. As the cashier was being paid, Lilly twirled out of the line snatching the fifth pretzel from the tray of already paid for pretzels and hopped back into her magic taxi. She hoped that the taxi might have left behind a note to cover the cost of the pretzel. As Lilly sat at the table, which dangled one meter above the floor, she began munching on the large pretzel. Then the magic taxi lifted itself up, taking Lilly and her pretzel to another destination. To Lilly's surprise when she landed, she had ended up back where she had found her magic taxi, in front of the posh shop, where her mother stood waiting for her to return. As she spotted her, Lilly ran over to her mum. She was so excited to tell her mum about her adventure.

The Fairies' Taxi
by Chloe Lennon aged 11

Ruby lived in the little town of Betws y Coed with her mum, dad, and little brother, Sam. They were always going on holiday and on outings with her parents' friends and Ruby loved it because she would get cakes, sweets, chocolate, new clothes, and much more. On the other hand, Sam hated it. All Sam wanted to do was play with his friends and go on holiday with his friends. Sam never used to mind it until one year he was invited to go to Spain with his best friend, Max, but his parents had said no because they were going on holiday with their friends to Greece. It was at that moment Sam decided he was going to do anything to make sure he didn't have to go. But that didn't work out for him and so he continued to try to change things. Last year he was going to try and make sure that they didn't go out for Ruby's 12th birthday to the steak hut, which they always went to because he knew that Ruby secretly didn't like steak which was why she always ordered the buffalo shrimps with ketchup and chips. As per usual they went anyway but it wasn't like any of the years before. No, it was very different…

They started the day off by her mum bringing Ruby breakfast in bed (pancakes with maple syrup, squirty cream, and strawberries which were her favourite) like every other year and then they went to Bounce Below with some of Ruby's friends for her party and they finished off the day by going to the steak hut with their parents' friends. Like every year Ruby's parents got a little bit drunk so they had to get a taxi home. But this taxi wasn't like a normal taxi. It was baby blue with stickers of rainbows and fairies on the side. They didn't care though they just got into the taxi ready to go home. But they went far from home.

As soon as they stepped into the taxi, they all fell straight asleep. When they woke up, they were lying in the middle of a light pink Delia in a field of beautiful, luscious flowers, shining, emerald green grass, and large, old oak trees that spread a huge canopy over half of the field. Going through the middle of the field was a sapphire blue river that shimmered in the sun and trickled slowly in between the large boulders that lay firmly in the riverbed. Ruby and Sam realised that their parents weren't there. They started to panic and when Ruby fell of the Delia, they realised that they had wings and could fly. They saw some other winged creatures heading towards the large oak tree, so they decided to follow them.

When they reached the oak tree, they were greeted by a cheerful, blonde fairy that was wearing a blue dress. The fairy said, "Welcome to fairy land! You have been chosen along with some other children to become fairies." She saw the panic that moved across their faces. "Don't worry about your parents they are nice and safe at home and won't even notice your gone. Please, follow the other fairies into the grand hall and form a straight line with them. There you will be judged to see if you are a water fairy like me, an animal fairy, a flower fairy, or a weather fairy judging by your hobbies and talents." With that, she flew away into the distance.

They did as the water fairy had instructed and there they had to wait in a long queue. When they finally reached the front, they had to fill in a questionnaire and try and complete loads of obstacles. Once they had completed this, they found out that Ruby was a water fairy and Sam was a weather fairy. They headed to their different fairy houses and had breakfast, then they had to complete the jobs that their house captains had told them to. Turned out the cheerful water fairy that greeted them was called Atlanta and Sam's house captain was a kind, but really strong boy called Storm. They were made to change their names, Ruby to Pearl and Sam to Thunder. Their life carried on like this for 2 years. Until one day they were told to go to the fairy queen, Alana. They were told that they were now going to be transported back to the real world as their time in the fairy world had come to an end, but they wouldn't remember anything. They weren't sure why the queen was doing this, but they had to obey. The next morning, they said goodbye to their friends and at the end of the day they flew into the magic taxi.

They woke up in their beds in their real house thinking that it was the day after Ruby's 12th birthday. No one had any idea about the magic taxi, fairy land, or Ruby and Sam's life as fairies.

The Tale of Lightning and Infinity
by Felix Russell aged 9

One day in 2090, Infinity and his sidekick Lightning were in Florida, swimming in their pool. Their house was as big as a cruise ship, they loved it. Just as Infinity was going to say, "this is the life." A siren broke out. Infinity and Lightning wasted no time, shared the same look, and clambered on their hover bikes. Zoom!

While they were riding, they realised that King Villain, the leader of all villains is trying to use his nuclear power weapon to disintegrate the world. Suddenly they hear a giant crash! A highway breaks in front of them, boom! Their hover bikes crash into the broken highway, so now their only option is to run. Lightning can run like his name. He sees that King Villain is destroying even more things, it won't be long until he destroys the whole world.

They see a gigantic, terrifying, beastly, radioactive Killing Machine. "Uhh..." Lightning says. "I think in exactly 5 seconds, this thing is going to blow. Blow up the world I mean," (he says all this in 1 second) ...4... the machine beeped. It started to glow .3... "Ma, ha, ha, ha." King Villain laughed. "You're back..." said Infinity... 2... "Yes, to blow up you and the world..." 1... The Killing Machine beeped for the last time. "I think we need to go back in tttiiiiiiimmmmme!!!"

"I'm setting us back for 2 days," says Infinity quickly. Then, they hear a humming noise, and suddenly they start swirling.
Crunch! Bang!! Boom!
Infinity sighs. "We have crashed landed on our roof."

"No matter," says Lightning triumphantly, "how about we steal the batteries from the nuclear power weapon, so that King Villain can't blow up the world?"

"Um, yeah I guess," mumbles Infinity.

"Well, let's go then," says Lightning.

"Hello, this is your Captain speaking. We have brought together a team of agents to stop King Villain dominating the world. We are on Starship 24, our personalised jet for all of us. Hope you enjoy your flight. Come to the Captain if you need anything." Says Captain Stealth the head agent. The team of agents includes Infinity, Lightening, Agent Super, Agent Sneaky, Agent Strong, all huddled together making a plan.

Captain Stealth pulls a switch, and they land. They jump off the speedy jet. Captain Stealth says his goodbyes and then suddenly in a blink, Starship 24 is only a memory... Everyone gets in their vehicles, Lightning and Infinity have a hoverbike each, Agent Super with a mini-jet, Agent Sneaky with a hover board, Agent Strong with 1000 mph taxi cab.

'Zoom, vroom, bang, and BOOM!' All of them are speeding to the killing machine. But what they don't know is that there are dangerous guards...

Scrreechhhh!!!! They halt all together. "Agent Sneaky, you're up," whispers Infinity. Agent Sneaky gets his sawing device, sticks it on the 'Killing Machine' and "boom!!" Agent Sneaky sneaks in and shuts down all the power so the siren won't go off when they steal the batteries. He sneaks out, running to the rest, "I'm ready!" he shouts.

Next up is Agent Strong, he crawls in the hole and realises that there is a giant barrier in front of him. "That's the job for me then!" he whispers to himself. He lifts the metal gate and can see the batteries. He runs back to where the others are.

Lightning and Agent Super are up next. They use their powers together to knock out all the guards and open the doors to the batteries. First Agent Super uses levitation on Lightning so that he can fly upwards, then Lightning uses super-speed so that he can strike through anything in his path. But suddenly he hears marching…

Zoom! Bang! Pow! Lightning is all on his own, fighting the marching robot guards.
"I need back up!". He calls on his mini phone.
"Coming right away," says Agent Strong, whilst picking up two robots, smashing them together, and throwing them at even more robots.
Fwooshhh!! "Hello, fellow friends," booms Agent Super, flying through the air, hurling laser beams at the robots.
"Ooh… don't forget about me." Agent Sneaky laughs and starts to throw dynamite everywhere. But where is Infinity??

"Guys they're closing in on us," says Agent Strong in a worried voice. "What do we do?"
Then suddenly all they can see is a very bright light, everywhere.
BOOM! Infinity uses his ultra-laser sword and stabs it into the ground, the sword causes beams of energy to race towards the enemy. Now all they can see is miles and miles of dead robots.
"Infinity!! you saved us," they all chimed together.
"Now everyone, we need to go and get the batteries." They clamber into the battery room, taking one each as they are very big and heavy. Suddenly all the lights went out.

The swirling starts again.

BOOM!! they land again… Back to the day that they started this time journey. Infinity dials 999 on his mini phone. "Hello, this is Infinity speaking." (Infinity knows the police) "Oh hello," the Police Sergeant says. "Could you go to State park beach?" asked Infinity.
"Yeah, sure we will be there in a bit."

Lightening and Infinity high-five each other, and once again clamber on their hover bikes. Vroom, vroom, vroom! they are off. This time they do NOT go down to the highway. They arrive at State Beach. All the police are there firing at the Killing Machine. …5… this time Infinity and Lightning do not worry about the siren and just wait…4… …3… .2…. 1 nothing happens. All they can hear is King Villain getting frustrated saying, "work stupid thing, do your job."
"Nope." Beeps the machine.
"King Villain you are officially arrested." Says the Police Sargent, and after that Lightning and Infinity lived happily ever after.

THE END

Imagination
by Freya Crump aged 10

"Mum there's one over there," exclaimed Joy.
"Come on quick!" Ivy ushered her daughter over and held her dark hand up to get the taxi's attention. Joy was still embarrassed that she had imagined a limo coming to get them, and earlier had shouted out about it, but she followed her mum all the same. The two clambered into the shiny, black London taxi and seated themselves awkwardly on the seats. They had hardly ever been in a taxi because they were extremely poor. Once the shopping bags had been stowed by Ivy's knees the driver jerked them forward and they were off.

"Thank you!" cooed Ivy minutes later, pulling out all the money from her battered purse and handing it to the driver. As soon as they had arrived at their tiny shack of a house, Ivy set about making dinner and Joy got out her sketchpad and began to draw. Joy and her mother were as different as mother and daughter could be. While Joy was fair-haired and full of imagination and kindness, Ivy was dark-haired and full of worry and misery. Joy resembled her dead father far more than her mother.

"Dinner is ready, Joy!" announced Ivy abruptly ten minutes later.
Joy knew it wouldn't be a feast as they had no money.
Being poor meant even everyday things like going to school was always a miserable affair for Joy. She was teased because of the pink dress that she wore every day and about how her and her mother were extremely poor. She didn't even have any friends to stand by her and make her feel better.

She slouched home miserably thinking about it all and imagining having a friend and not being teased. As she stared at the bustling London road her imagination whirring, she saw something that made her stop dead. Right in front of her dazzling blue eyes was a taxi like no other. It was a bright yellow colour with golden wings sprouting out of the roof and it was the size of a limousine. It was that same taxi she had imagined the previous day after her and her mum had gone shopping. But somehow, it didn't look as though it was her imagination. She gazed open-mouthed and then deciding on the spot, flagged it down. The yellow taxi halted in front of her and she saw through the window that the driver was also open-mouthed. Suddenly, the doors banged open of their own accord and the driver murmured, "Hop in," to Joy. Joy suddenly noticed that he wasn't much older than her. This puzzled her, how could someone around the age of twelve be a taxi driver? She sat down in the passenger seat next to him where he had gestured. The inside of the taxi was just as amazing as the outside. There was a fridge, toilet, shower, bedroom and much, much more. Following her gaze, he smiled, "It's not what you'd imagine an ordinary taxi to be like is it?" he asked.

"Not exactly, no."

"What's your name, miss?"

"Joy, what's yours?"

"Isaac."

The two children whiled away most of their magical journey happily talking about the nonsense children talk about. Isaac hadn't even asked Joy where she needed to go but she wasn't fussed about that because for once in her life she felt like she had made a friend and was even more happy than normal about it.

"So how did you get the taxi?" asked Joy as they flew through wisps of cloud. Joy had got used to how it flew now but it had come as a huge shock when the taxi had first suddenly shot upwards.

"My dad made it, it flies by itself and is powered by the strongest magic ever."

"Which is?"

"Imagination of course!"

After several days of this amazing life, Joy spotted a scared rabbit on the ground with a car edging ever closer to it. Her heart began to pound with worry for the rabbit. "Get down there, Isaac!" she commanded urgently, "There's a rabbit down there about to be squashed!"

Immediately Isaac ushered the car downwards and Joy got out just in time. She grabbed the rabbit and zoomed away from the car. She looked down at the poor rabbit and felt her stomach drop. She was no longer holding a rabbit, but a man and they were no longer in the street but in a cage. She let go of the man and let out an ear-splitting scream, that although loud could not carry to anyone that might help. Meanwhile, in the taxi a horror-struck Isaac was stuck down on the ground unable to move the taxi and unable to find help as few people could actually see it. His heart was racing, and his mind was blank, but suddenly something dark brown flew past his head and perched its massive body on his shoulder. His mouth fell open it was his pet golden eagle! "Are you thinking what I think you're thinking, Goldie?" He asked it slowly. The eagle nodded its beak in answer and began to fly with Isaac in its claws. Isaac's face split into a smile, "Let's go then!" he bellowed happily, they were going to save Joy!

"Is that it, Goldie?" he questioned as they flew through the sky, "Is that Dr Disaster's hide out?" the bird blinked to agree. The two glided down smoothly and landed with a bump. Chains covered the entire place, but Isaac was the son of the most powerful magician so could blast this apart with a click of his fingers. Once he and his eagle were inside, a small hand entwined itself into his and a voice whispered in his ear, "Isaac, how did you get in?" He knew that voice! "How did you get out of the cage he puts everyone in?" "Magic, the most powerful magic; imagination of course!" she replied. "Well, come on Joy, we gotta go!" Joy's arms were wrapping around him in thanks and he hugged her back.

He had saved her.

But this was only the beginning!

25

Escape
by Jessica Thomas aged 13

Bob Thomas had always loved magic. His long-life dream was to travel to another universe. He had always been a wild, bad-mannered person with a fat, glaring face and spiky, rotten teeth. His friends saw him as a bit of a devil.

One day his dream came true…

He had bought his first taxi for his new business.

It didn't seem quite right, when he got in, there was golden dust on the seats, and a note saying "if you pull this lever you may never come back…"

Bob looked out of the window and reflected on his calm surroundings. The sun shone down on him and for once in his lifetime he felt peaceful. This was his chance to escape this world.

Then he saw something in the distance, or rather someone. It was the figure of Lee Parker. Lee was a small sweet, little girl, with long golden hair. Bob stepped outside his taxi and Lee came closer, he could see a glint in her eye, she looked deadly. Lee was a nasty piece of work.

Bob gulped. He was not prepared for someone like Lee. He was not used to people not being terrified of him.

She said, very aggressively, "I despise you, but I want a magical taxi ride."

Bob looked back, confused.

She whispered, "yes, I know your secret I've been watching this city and that car just appeared!"

Still stood next to his magical taxi Bob said. "Ok if I must, I will, but let me warn you this other universe may be very different, and we may never come back."

They looked at each other with weird feelings, like two powerless, people at the start of a very exhilarating magical trip. They both carefully climbed into the taxi and fastened their seatbelts, ready…

Bob pulled the lever slowly; all went still, and nothing happened.
BANG!
Lee and Bob are flung forward. Golden dust flew all around them. Like a dream.
Suddenly…
They landed on the hard, cold, ground. The sky is filled with fluffy pink candyfloss clouds. The ground glows. They both jumped up. Lee straightened her fancy blue shirt with her small hands. Bob suddenly jumped backwards. Lee looked forward, and they both ran away, because what they saw is not going to be nice to them!
Behind them stomped a large fierce red beast. His claws were like razors. He was larger than an elephant. He had a large mouth that could eat ten double-decker buses in one gulp. He stomped loudly towards them; his two large legs powered him quickly towards the two intruders. His huge mouth snapped at the large trees breaking them in half, he cleared a path for himself. Nothing would stand in his way, not a tree, a river, but, they thought, the sea might. The sea behind them was deep, dark, and cold but if Lee and Bob could swim to the other side of the island, they might be able to escape…
They both yanked off their shoes and ran across the hot, sandy beach. The waves splashed their feet as they ran into the sea. Lee found herself waist-deep in the cold water, she picked up her feet and swam for her life. Meanwhile, Bob was struggling to keep going, he lifted his feet, but he started to sink… The beast was gaining on them, he stomped through the water, the waves got higher on him and he started to turn back slowly, but Bob started to drown. Lee tried to swim back against the tide to save him, but she took in a gulp of the salty sea water and started to choke. Who could save them …?
The red monster turned back; he saw that both intruders were drowning. So, his mighty legs powered him forward towards the deepest part of the sea. He

lowered his big, muscly red head down into the water. He opened his mouth, showing his large, shiny, white teeth. He put his head under the water. Lee was boiling with fear, the beast grabbed her and snapped her up in one big gulp.

Now the beast turned to the fat-faced Bob Parker, it licked its red lips, it was ready for its second meal of the day. It opened its mouth as wide as a bus. It snaped up Bob. Then it left the deep blue water and wandered away. Bob and Lee will never come back again. The taxi did warn them.

The Magic Map
by Siya Patel aged 12

My name is Phoebe Allen. I have two best friends: Indigo (we call her Indie) and Hannah. It was the summer holidays and as usual, nothing was happening. Until that one, typical summer's day…

The day started off fine – my 6- year- old brother (Buddy) woke me up by bouncing on my bed, the birds were chirping in the early morning air and the delicious aroma of sausages was coming from the kitchen. As I made my way downstairs, my father greeted me at the landing - "Phoebe, my boss just dropped off an old taxi – it's in the garage. He'll come back and take it at the end of the day but make sure you're careful if you go down there." My dad works in a taxi company, so this didn't surprise me.
"No worries Dad, me, Indie, and Hannah are going to the park today."
"Great, have fun!" he replied…

After breakfast Indie and Hannah and I, were just about to leave for the park when all of a sudden, I remembered I needed to fetch our neighbours dog's food bowl – I had been looking after him the day before but had forgotten to give the bowl back to his owner. "Guys, I'll be out in a sec, I've got to get something from the garage," I told my two waiting friends; I knew Indie was usually quite impatient.
"We'll come with you, you know how impatient I am!" replied Indie, as if she has read my mind! "Ok then, come on!" 5 minutes later, we were in my gloomy garage, I've got to admit that it isn't my favourite place in the house! Cobwebs litter the ceiling; the walls creak as if they're suffering and the flickering lights utterly creep me out. The old and battered taxi that my dad had mentioned was parked neatly in front of us. "Hang on a sec…" I said, rummaging about for the food bowl.

"Phoebe, what's this?" I heard Hannah ask from behind me.

Not looking back, I replied, "Oh, that's a taxi that my dad's boss dropped off. It's just here for the day," thinking that's what she was asking about.

"No, this scroll in the back of the taxi," Hannah replied. Confused, I turned around, looking in the direction she was pointing in. "Oh, I'm sure my dad must have overlooked it, it's in the back after all," I said, wondering what on earth it was doing in the back of a taxi. Indie (being the curious person she was), pulled it out of the taxi, and when she did, a note fluttered to the floor.

"What's this?" queried Hannah. Picking it up, she read aloud,

"No need for a key.

There's only three.

Tap three times for a ride in this magic taxi.

When you choose your destination.

Make sure you beware.

That you might not like who you meet there!

Finally, ensure you remember that only one chance you may have,

to ride this magical cab!!!"

"What on earth is this about?" questioned Hannah, speaking for the three of us; we were all as confused as each other. What did this mean? Was this really a magical taxi? Who would we meet where?

"I reckon there's only one way to find out," grinned Indie reading my mind again.

"Are you out of your mind? We can't just go riding about in some old taxi! Goodness knows where we might end up!" said Hannah, looking at Indie as if she was crazy.

"Come on, Hannah, what's the harm in just tapping three times and seeing where it takes us?" argued Indie. As Hannah opened her mouth to argue, I stepped between them.

"Listen, guys, the rhyme says, 'there's only three' and that must be referring to us – it's like we're meant to ride in the taxi!" I said excitedly, wondering what on earth this could mean. "Let's just tap three times and see what happens. I mean, when will we ever get a chance to ride a magic taxi again Hannah?" I continued.

"Fine, but at the slightest sign of trouble, we'll jump straight out," she replied, glaring at me and Indie.

"Got it! I've got a feeling this is going to be fun, right Indie? Indie?" I looked behind me – Indie had disappeared. The scroll was on the floor. Where could she have gone in such a small place? Suddenly, a banging sound flooded through the garage. And it seemed to be coming from the magic taxi! Turning around, I saw Indie excitedly banging on the window of the cab. "Tap three times on the scroll!" she mouthed. Hesitantly, Hannah picked up the tattered scroll, and together, we tapped once, twice, and three times...

As I opened my eyes, I found myself inside a taxi – how had that happened? The inside of the taxi was exactly like the outside – filthy and stained. However, when I looked at the scroll in my hand, I found it had turned into a map! The weird thing was that the places on the map were absurd and sounded like they had been made up! "Land of lost and found," said Hannah, examining the map closely. Suddenly, with no warning whatsoever, the taxi gave a massive jolt and before we knew it, we were whizzing through the air at what seemed like a 1000mph! All that was outside of the taxi was a mysterious grey fog and as we were thrown about, Hannah kicked me on the side and Indie flopped on top of me, I screamed in terror. Then, just as quickly as it had started, the taxi stopped. Silence pervaded the air. Nothing. That was until the door flew open and we were thrown out onto the ground by some invisible force! The taxi then seemed to sigh and settled down in front of us. "Oh my god! What just happened?" breathed Hannah, as bewildered as all of us. As I was about to reply, a kindly looking lady came up to us. "Why you're in the Land of Lost and Found!" she cried. 'Well that was something', I thought. All around us were piles and piles of junk – diaries, socks, pens, hair clips. "Come, I'll take you to my house," she said. Thinking of nothing better to do, we heaved ourselves up and followed her through the abnormal junkyard. As we approached what seemed to be the only house for miles, we walked through her front lawn (which looked as if it could do with a good trim) and through the wooden door. The lock clicked behind us… She led us to a small sitting room with just a little red sofa and a single wooden chair. Before we could say anything, she transformed into a horrible looking witch with bubbling warts and more wrinkles than skin. 'Oh no, what have we gotten ourselves into?' I thought, remembering the click of the lock. Cackling, she shouted "Oh, you silly things, did you actually think I was a kind, old lady? "I'm going to keep you trapped here forever and take that magical taxi of yours for myself! Excuse me while I fetch a spell that will turn you into cats! I like cats." Laughing hysterically, she swept off, clicking the lock behind her.

"Now what?" cried Hannah, tears filling her eyes. Indie sat down on the sofa. Suddenly she cried, "OW!!!" Looking at what she has just sat on, she pulled out a bottle that said 'TELEPORTING POTION, DRINK'… "Bingo!!!" I cried. Hurriedly, we grabbed the bottle, and each took a little swig. "The taxi!" cried Indie. But it was too late…

I opened my eyes wearily for the second time that day and found myself in our garage with the taxi by my side – it must have sped home after us! "Phew, I thought we'd lost it!" cried Hannah. Hugging each other, memories flooded back about what had happened. What a day! 'Only one chance'. I remembered the note had read. "We won't be able to do that again," I said sadly. Oh well, what an adventure we'd had!!!

The Rat's Revenge
by Ibraham Ali Azhar aged 10

Rat was done with life.

His brother had gone missing as had so many others.

Now a cat had found its way to the sewers and had almost eaten the elders. He would not have it anymore.

He jumped up the ladder and went away without permission; he was on a quest to punish humanity and all animals. A thing that no rat had dared to do before. A quest to spread a disease, normally a special rat disease happened every one hundred years but this one happened out of sequence. He thought he should make them call it leptospirosis. Rat ran into a taxi cab and hid in the glove compartment. He hoped nobody searched in here for paperwork or something. He found some old cheese and saved it partly because he was not hungry, and mostly because he was afraid that they would hear his chewing. When Rat calmed down, he realized he could not go back. All his anger was overwhelmed by one emotion. Fear. Suddenly, a low deep voice entered the car. It said, "A-rat-a-tat-a!" and for one horrible moment he thought he had been discovered but then he realized he heard it a lot around the sewer exit and it was definitely a catchphrase and his worried feelings left him.

Suddenly he realized that they were in the magic world; it meant this was The Cab, the special taxi cab that is magical, and that comes every century. Why had it come early this year? He had no time to think because the next moment he heard the deep voices again. He jumped out of the glove compartment. He spat out masticated cheese in fear. He needed to find the button to get out. He saw a button that had been told about, it had been described so many times in stories told by the elders. A red shaped button with a rat on it. He stamped his foot on it. It was not as he thought; instead of a door opening, he teleported to somewhere. It looked like a dungeon.

Suddenly he saw a cell. To his horror inside it was his... brother and all the rats that had gone missing. That's why the taxi cab had come early. It was to steal rats. It had turned against them. Now he was fuelled with rage. Suddenly, from nowhere a cat pounced from the shadows, and he was frozen in fear. The cat knew he was there. He had to run but he couldn't leave the other rats here. Then he remembered! he had a fake rubber rat! He did the most impulsive thing ever. Rat threw his backpack at the cat to distract it, he jumped on its back and threw the winded up mouse under its nose. He grabbed the backpack and crashed the cat into the wall. It made a massive hole. The cat was unconscious. The rats had time to escape. He led the rat army to the magical cab. The humans were coming. The rat army had the strength of numbers so they could easily overpower the humans. The rats knocked them to the floor and quickly ran into the magical cab and they said goodbye to the treacherous and magical world. On their way back, Rat couldn't help being anxious. He had broken many of the elders' laws and because of this, he was sure to be exiled. Much to his surprise, he was welcomed by many multicoloured streamers and requests for autographs, but Rat still had not done what he wanted to. The next day he asked for an audience with the elders and he got it. He asked if he could get a new rat virus in the world. The elders confirmed that they now had control of the taxi again and they granted him permission. Rat could not believe his ears. He pinched himself to see if he was dreaming. He was not. He had been granted permission. Time for another adventure.

Taxi Ride to Destiny
by Amelie Lee aged 10

She sat down with a sigh. Another curious child had disappeared from a taxi. This was the fourth one this week. Where did they go? Nobody knew. Grace decided she needed to investigate. It's not normal for so many people to go missing in such a short amount of time.

Grace arrived in the city with her notebook and a pen. She sat on a bench on the side of the road and watched the people that got into taxis. Everyone she saw was described in her notebook.

However, when she read the newspaper, none of the people she saw had gone missing, which was strange. All of the children that went missing were in the area she had been searching. There was only one way she could find out what was going on; she had to go in a taxi.

The car that pulled up was as black as night and the windows were completely blacked out so the outside world couldn't see in. Slightly hesitantly, Grace opened the door and climbed inside.

Suddenly, Grace was plunged into darkness. She was plummeting to the ground, falling faster and faster, her heartbeat quickening every second. Before long, the curious girl hit the ground. Strangely, it didn't hurt her at all, which was weird, considering the height she fell from.

She must have been unconscious because the next thing she remembered was checking her watch and it being 10 pm. Quietly and carefully, Grace stood up and began to explore.

There was a huge iron door with an impregnable lock used for keeping it secure, but it wasn't locked. It swung open and she reluctantly walked through it. All of a sudden, the 12-year-old was blinded by a bright white light. Stood before her were the 4 children that had gone missing! Behind them was a tall dark shape, looking down on them.

"Hello, I am Star, leader of this group. Only the most inquisitive children are taken into this group where they find out their magical abilities." said the dark shape, it stepped into the light and Grace saw it was a tall woman. The first child was a boy around the age of 10 with red hair and freckles. "I'm Zach and my power is telepathy." The second child was a girl around the age of 8 with black hair. "My name is Sophie, and my magical power is telekinesis." The third child was a girl around 16 with blue hair. "The name's Chloe and my power's shapeshifting." The fourth child was a boy around 12 with blonde hair and blue eyes. "Hello there, what's your name? I'm Daniel and my power is super strength."

"Hi Daniel, I'm Grace," she replied.

Star stepped in-between them and said, "Let's get on with finding your power, shall we?"

After 10 minutes of walking, they arrived in a room with a white light and white walls. There were many strange-looking devices: a large glass case with metal bars all around the inside of it; a table with two grey headbands connected to wire; thick bars of osmium; and a zombie-like creature in a glass cage.

It took 2 hours for Grace to get through all of the tests until there was only one left: and it involved the zombie. "You must touch the zombie and if you see a vision tell me. If not, then we have chosen the wrong person and you don't have any magical abilities." Star informed her. Grace reached out and touched the zombie. She saw a lightning bolt shoot into the building and destroy the creature. "I-I-I saw a vision. I-it died."

The children gawped in the doorway. "She's the leader child. She's the most magical child of this generation," Star said, and they all gasped in unison. "Wait what?" Grace asked in utter confusion. "What are you talking about? I've never heard of that!"

Chloe said crossly, "Well, you didn't know magical powers existed either so that's no surprise."

"And you did?" Grace retorted. Chloe walked away, mumbling nasty things inaudibly. Without saying anything, Grace reached out and touched the older girl's arm. She whispered in Chloe's ear, "I know how you die." The 16-year-old gave her a death glare as she walked away.

"Wait, she's seen a human vision! That means she's immortal too!" Sophie cried from the doorway. "Doesn't it Star?"

Star replied," Indeed it does. You, Grace Marshall, are a very lucky girl. You are the only person ever to be magically talented enough to have this power. And I get to teach you! Take that sister!"

2 days later...

The group was eating in the breakfast room when Grace said. "Hey Star, why is the transportation device to get here a taxi?"

Chloe gulped down her food and said "So, only 2 days ago you found out you were the most magical child in the universe and all you want is to know about is Star's dumb story about a taxi! No offence Star."

"None taken, don't worry- I'm never offended. Well, Grace Marshall, the reason you were transported here in a taxi is not so simple. There was no sole reason I chose a taxi; it was a combination of many smaller reasons. The first was simply because it is a mundane object. Nobody would suspect a child getting into a taxi.

Secondly, taxis have always been my favourite form of transport. I don't know why, but they have fascinated me since I was young. Taxis always made me feel mature, going out in a car all by myself, it put me ahead of my sister.

Thirdly (the main reason), is a story. It all started when my great-grandmother was young and very rich. It was the first discovery of magic powers in children, and she was asked by an old powerful woman to start a magical school. She agreed to use her wealth to help create a school based around the woman's teachings. On the first day of the school, the woman asked my great-grandmother, how will we transport the children here? My great-grandmother didn't know. They sat for a while pondering what they could-" she stopped abruptly. Knock. Knock. Knock. Nobody did anything. The door opened and a dripping wet figure came towards them with its face hooded.

The group huddled together nervously, awaiting their fate. The figure lifted up the wet hood, revealing a man, he looked Grace in the eyes.

"My child, I was devastated when I had to leave you on the orphanage doorstep, but I always knew you would get back into magic."

Grace spoke with utter confusion, "Father? I thought you were dead. Why did you leave me when I was so young?"

"I left you because your mother had disappeared, and I was an emotional mess. I wasn't ready to look after a child. When I was ready, I couldn't find you but now I have, and I can finally be a proper father!"

Grace was so happy.

She and her father opened the door wide to see the sunset. They walked out, hand in hand, bonding after 12 years of being apart.

Ava, Monty and the Magic Taxi
by Maya Walther aged 10

In a town called Sorrow where happiness was unknown lived two children called Ava and Monty. One cloudy day as the children were strolling miserably through Tearful Lane, they noticed something odd. A bright, yellow taxi was parked on the road in between the usual unwashed black taxis.

Ava pulled at her older brother's grey school jumper.
"Monty why is a yellow taxi parked on Tearful Lane?" she asked him curiously.
Monty stopped and thought for a moment and then he said, "I don't know Ava and we'll be late for school if you keep stopping and asking questions."
"Sorry Monty," she said, and the children continued their stroll to school.

When they arrived at Bitter Primary school the children sensed something peculiar was up. Their headteacher Mrs Grey was not there to wish them bad luck. Instead, a pink unicorn dressed in a purple bow tie greeted them with a warm and pleasant smile and wished them good luck instead of bad. The classrooms did not have any teachers but instead fairies and nymphs!
"This is all a dream," Monty said to his sister.
Ava shrugged. But on her face, her frown turned upside down.

Five minutes later an odd sound like an untuned violin and a boat horn mixed together rang throughout the school.
"Lesson time!" said a squeaky voice and the children ran to their classrooms. But then as they entered the classrooms that same squeaky voice rang throughout the school again.

"Home time!" and suddenly all the children's faces wore the same upside-down frown Ava had worn earlier.

They all ran out of the school gates and entered the taxis that were waiting for them, all assigned by their parents.
Emmy and Kemmy however were still fighting over who the watermelon lip gloss belonged to and so the quarrelling twins entered separate cabs.
When Ava and Monty appeared outside there was only the yellow taxi, they had seen that morning, left.
"We'll walk," Monty said.
"No," and Ava pulled her brother towards the yellow taxi.
Ava opened the taxi door and stood back, allowing her brother to enter first.
"Let's get this done with as soon as possible," he muttered to himself and Ava heaved her older brother in.
She shut the door and glanced at her brother.
"Um well...Mister I'd like to go to No.31, Tearful Lane, please?"
The driver didn't respond for a while.
But at last, he said," Adventure is the only option."
Ava shrugged and looked around for the driver.
"I can't see you," she replied at last.
"I am the taxi. The magic taxi, so hop in for adventure, and away we go!"
The children buckled up.
"Ready?" asked the taxi.
And before her brother could say 'no' Ava shouted, "YES!"

Then the children zoomed through Sorrow until suddenly they had left the ground.
They were flying. They had entered a magic, flying taxi.
"Oh my!" exclaimed Ava.

This was definitely the best taxi ride she had ever had but Monty didn't agree. Was a taxi allowed to fly? Were they being tricked into riding the taxi so they could be taken to a villain's evil lair?

Then all of a sudden, the taxi dropped a little.

"One of you isn't happy so my tire burst."

Ava glanced at Monty and the two braced themselves for a crash landing.

Bang!

When they got up from the crash, they glanced around them.

"Taxi, where are we?" asked Ava.

The taxi glanced around.

"Colourful crowds of people, stalls filled with delicious food and fine silks. Children, I think we are in Jollyfields, your neighbouring town."

For the first time ever, Monty jumped up in the air smiling.

"Taxi," he said, "Please show us around!"

Ava gave him a dirty look.

"We can't! The poor taxi burst a tire. No thanks to you!" she moaned.

"Right." he gulped.

"Actually, there is one way you can help me," said Taxi.

They turned round and looked at him hopefully.

"Try to find one girl in town called Joy. She'll help."

Monty raised an eyebrow but as he did his little sister Ava tugged at his backpack, and soon they were off exploring the streets of Jollyfields.

"Wow!" Ava exclaimed pulling her brother over to look at the purple teddy bear she had spotted.

She reached into her bag and pulled out a coin. She handed it to the lady who was selling the bears and they continued their search for Joy.

A while later they spotted a girl with pigtails.

Ava asked her if she was Joy and she got a reply.

"I'm Joy!" she said.

The children smiled.

"I hope you're not taking me to a yellow taxi though."

Ava and Monty glanced at each other.

"Um...well we are," Monty said.

"Oh, so I suppose he wants you to get me to break the curse I put on him."

Ava and Monty were amazed.

"Well, I'll break it. You are the first riders to come to me and ask me to break it."

The children jumped for joy.

When they got back to the taxi, they watched him transform into a young boy just a few years older than Monty. Joy told them his name was Jack and that they both were brother and sister but one day Jack turned mean and cruel and so she put a curse on him. But over the years he turned nicer, still, no one helped to break the curse and that was where they came in.

They all glanced at Jack who was blushing with embarrassment.

"One question," Monty said as they started to walk back to Sorrow, "Why were you a taxi?"

"Well, that was just my sister being weird!" Jack said.

When they got home, they shared their story and soon everyone learned that kindness was the way forward. So, Sorrow was changed to Kindness and their lives changed forever.

The M Taxi
by Smriti Saraf aged 8

I whistled for the drab dirty taxi that nobody else had wanted, it was raining, and I had no jacket on, so I was getting soaked and I was left with the worst taxi of all. Its sign said it was "The M taxi" but I didn't care I just wanted to stop getting wet.

Everyone else had shiny brand-new taxis that I bet were polished every day, with smooth leather seats, smart drivers wearing suits and posh hats that had a white stripe on the bottom. I opened the wet door with bits of paint chipped off and saw that the seats were disgusting! They had crumbs and old crisp bags that had been stepped on, wet patches that were green, and worst of all, there was a half-eaten sandwich that was so old it had mould all over it! I tried to sit in the cleanest spot but really there wasn't one, so I tried to squeeze myself up so that I wouldn't be touching anything, who knows what the wet patches were? But really, I ended up half standing. I didn't say anything though. We started going…

I looked out of the window and I saw a…, no! I was just imagining things, wasn't I?

I never thought I would say this, but it looked like a magical forcefield! I couldn't believe my eyes! It was tremendous! I realised the front of the car was slowly disappearing! I felt like I was being sucked into a mysterious magical who knows what? (which I was!).

I poked my head over to the front seat. The driver looked as if this was perfectly normal! What an insane driver this fellow must be! I noticed that the whole car had transformed around me into an elegant car fit for royalty! The car was polished and shiny which reflected the sunlight that glistened beautifully, and the seats were made from velvet. I was amazed! I had witnessed something wonderful. I excitedly but carefully stepped out of the car and… We were in a completely different dimension! The sun was shining bright and the ground had grassy green meadows that little baby lambs sprinted across, the houses were bright and colourful with lovely flowers planted near them. It was marvellous, just marvellous! I looked at the taxi driver and he gave me a wink. I was speechless, I honestly didn't know what to say!

Now I realise why the cab is called the M taxi; it stands for magical. The next day when the driver took me home, I told lots of people about the great thing that happened to me, but everyone thought I was lying. After all, you probably wouldn't believe it unless you experience it for yourself. I never will forget that day. And I will never stop believing in magic.

Never judge a book by its cover.

The Taxi of The Huehounds
by Arnav Kasireddy aged 12

The acrid smell of the polluted air that repleted all over the crumbling building around me suffused my lungs. The clock was ticking second by second not showing any mercy. I had such a huge meeting tomorrow and somehow, I managed to oversleep on the train. Why doesn't anything go how I want it to?

As soon as I exited the station, I frantically started looking for taxis. I ran all over the place like I was mad, searching until an old yellow taxi came to a screeching halt next to the path that I was standing on, it splashed me with polluted raindrops from a large puddle. I stood there, startled, and very dismayed. The cold water took me by surprise; I shivered as it soaked through my clothes and trickled down my skin. I took a moment to examine the exterior of the vehicle that did this to me. Its odious sight was distasteful. I stared at the old hunk of rusty metal sheets, which seemed fused together crudely. I saw the rubber tires sagging under the weight of the body, ready to crumble at any moment; they were begging to be relieved of their job.

I quickly pounded on the window not being hesitant of the poor condition the taxi was in. I knew this was my only chance to get to the hotel in time to have enough rest for tomorrow's big day.

I shuddered as I entered the mechanical scrapheap. I could see the man's face through the rearview mirror. It wasn't too visible; however, he had dark brown unkempt hair and an air of nastiness. There were two tiny dark slits in the mass of hair that I managed to spot, where the man's eyes were most likely situated. In a voice that was edged with evil, he asked me, where I wanted to go. I was scared. Scared enough to forget about the fact that the driver ignorantly splashed water on me with his taxi. How could this world bear such a wicked and sinister man? Eventually, summoning my courage, I managed to tell the driver where to go.

The satnav showed that it would take three hours to arrive at the hotel. The time was already 10 pm so I realized that I should just sleep on the ride. However, I couldn't trust the sinister taxi driver. He constantly kept on looking at me from the rear-view mirror. I decided that I should just waste time on my phone because it was obvious that the driver wasn't a chatty type of guy.

Just as I was putting my hand into my bag, the obnoxious man said that he was taking a shortcut because there was a traffic jam on the motorway. I didn't feel too comfortable, but it was already eleven-thirty. I told him that was just fine and then he gave the most nasty, psychopathic laugh I'd ever heard. I started rethinking my decision. I'd rather be a few hours late to the hotel than be kidnapped in the middle of the night by a sketchy looking driver.

I started to think that I was just overreacting and that the driver was probably just tired. But we both know that I just thought that for reassurance. And then, suddenly, the phone that was secure in my hand slipped out and landed under the seat. I took off my seatbelt and bent to grab my phone. And when I eventually grasped it, the no battery symbol came up on the screen. Oh no!

The man took a right onto a bumpy, rocky road. If I wasn't creeped out a moment ago, I sure was now! All I could feel was the soft cotton of my suit rubbing against the rough leather that the driver called "seats".

We entered a forest, the huge trees watched above us like gods. I couldn't see anyone around us. Only a few luminous glows in the bushes presumably nocturnal animal's eyes as they scavenged for prey.

As we got deeper and deeper into the woods, the rocky terrain also got more uncomfortable. Until suddenly the car came to a stop! As I got out looking for clues as to why the taxi came to a halt, I realized that a tire had popped! Just then, the driver came up behind me and stated that he hadn't even brought a spare tire! I had enough! This guy was just wrong.

I ran away from him and the taxi as fast as I could! Suddenly, my watch started beeping! It was midnight. At that moment, I heard a howl! I never knew there were werewolves in the forest!

I turned around, not knowing why! I started running back to the taxi. I wouldn't let myself turn around. My fear was taking over me!

Then my hair started to grow, and my body started to get bigger and bigger until my clothes ripped into shreds.

I came face to face with the taxi driver. His teeth were bigger, and his look was completely different.

And out came the word, "huehound" from his and my mouth at the same time...

The train bounced on the tracks, startled, I looked around.

Oh no! I'd overslept on the train again due to my dream! I was doomed for the meeting tomorrow!

Madison and the Magic Taxi Cab
by Abbie Clarke aged 11

It was another dreary, windy day for Madison. Madison thought that every day when she walked out of her boring house, into a boring taxi cab to her boring work. But little did she know that she was very wrong!

Madison walked over to the little short taxi driver Tim. Tim gave her the usual morning smile and a cup of tea.

But there was more to the short, chubby little man than Madison thought. What she didn't know was that Tim was a wizard and lived in a hole in the ground. Tim never told anyone. It was his biggest secret.

They set off towards Madison's office and then suddenly the cab gave a bump.

"NOOOOO." shouted Tim

"What's happening?" protested Madison

"Umm slight issue," said Tim.

Suddenly they landed with a bump into the ground, Madison looked around in amazement and wondered why Tim was looking extremely flustered.

All of a sudden, a stout woman dressed in a red dress, with a pink apron shuffled out from one of the many doors in the walls.

"What you are doing bringing non-magic people down here Tim?" said the stout woman.

Madison looked at Tim and the stout woman in wonder.

"MAGIC?" she exclaimed

"Yes of course dear, we are magic folk."

"Wow, I didn't know that kind of stuff was real," Madison said excitedly.

"Now that you know I suppose you can have a look around," said Tim

"Oh, thank you," said Madison

She watched the pair scoot round the corner and wondered how on earth in this boring life, there was this, hidden below the surface.

She decided she would have a look around. She decided to take the first door on the left. She pulled down the shiny door handle which felt surprisingly silky as she pulled it open.

Madison walked In and all she saw in front of her were bottles and jars and trinkets of all sorts surrounding the room. There were potions galore! Blue, pink, yellow, orange, every colour you could possibly imagine. You name a colour it was there. It was amazing. As much as she knew she should not, she wanted to try the surprisingly sweet-scented blue potion.

She flicked off the brown cap and it scooted across the floor. She lifted the potion from the counter and held it to her lips.

She didn't bother to read the instruction label at the back of the bottle which read, 'Turn into a rabbit potion'. She swished it around her mouth and then swallowed. It was like something she had never tried before. Sweet and sour at the same time.

Suddenly she felt funny, almost like she was shrinking. She held a hand up to her face and saw hair. She tried to scream but all that was heard was a funny grunting noise. She looked behind her and saw a furry, bushy tail. It then sunk in that the potion had turned her into a rabbit. She knew she should start to look for a potion that would turn her normal again.

Eventually, she found a green slimy potion labelled 'Human features will return'.

She held the potion up to her rather furry lips and swigged the potion. It was disgusting. But after a relieved sigh she had turned back to normal.

She walked out of the room and decided to move onto the next one. This room was rather peculiar. It had little keys everywhere. But not just your normal old keys. Winged keys, flying keys, whizzing around the room. She tried to grasp one but all she felt was air. These things were so extremely fast. She realised that she would never be able to catch them so gave up and wandered out.

The next door was different from the rest. This one was purple and curtained as if no one wanted to go in there. Madison grasped the handle of the door which was slippery and cold as if it hadn't been touched in years. She entered the room and as she walked in, she let out a loud gasp.

The walls were peeling and there were ripped book pages covered in what looked like mud and dirt all over the floor. The worst of all was the fact that there was blood dripping from the ceiling. She turned round to walk out as she'd certainly seen enough. As she turned, she realised here was a sign on the inside of the door. She read aloud to herself

'Dear witches and wizards of the land off Wizardgamet,

This is where the war of wizards took place, hence the mess,

Please do not enter this room unless instructed to.

Head of Wizardgamet

Tim'

She quickly left the room.

The war of wizards sounded cool to her. Anyway, she continued her journey around this magical underground world.

She came to the next door and entered. Inside this room was a rather small yet tidy kitchen. There was a round table and mushroom stools. Tiny cupboards with dinky little teacups and plates. She liked this room, yet she found herself eager to get out and explore more.

She came out and saw the next door, she pulled open the handle which was extremely light weight. She wowed in astonishment as she saw what was inside. There were thousands, maybe even millions of little fairy doors everywhere. She decided to knock on one to see what would happen.

She was curious to see if these doors were truly only for decoration or if real-life little fairies lived here. She knocked and there was no reply but heard a rather weird shuffling noise. She decided to move on to the next door.

This door was a rather pale blue, almost white coloured. As soon as she touched the handle, she immediately felt like she was being transported.

She felt herself give a yawn and stretch and opened her eyes. She was back in Tim's cab.

It had all been a dream!

The Game
by Suleman aged 9

One cloudy, winter afternoon Bob was heading home from school.
He got in a taxi and while the driver was driving him to his house Bob played on his tablet.
He was playing a game called 'Block Crafting'. It was a game where everything was block-like, even your character!
The driver dropped him under a dim lamp, a few yards away from his house. Just as he was walking, his tablet started glowing and everything went black. When he opened his eyes, he saw that his body was a slim rectangle, he looked up and all the trees were made out of wood and leaf blocks. He realised he was inside the game, his tablet was still in his block-like hand, but it was glowing magically.
He knew what he had to do.
He went and built a house for protection, with a bookshelf and a bed and a warm oven to cook.

The next day Bob accidently pressed a button on his tablet, and he was thrown like a flying rock out of the game. He found himself back on the dimly lit street near his home. He walked to his house feeling relieved as he thought he would be trapped in the game forever.
He decided he would be careful when pressing strange buttons on his tablet. For the next few days he didn't use his tablet at all then one day he thought his tablet would be back to normal so he went on it but again he was sucked in, "not again," he said.
He found himself inside his small square block house.
Bob made an axe out of stone and wood and he went out to check the land around him, he found a colourful village surrounded by a yellow corn field

that gave him some seeds when he dug in the earth. He also found some pumpkin seeds. Lucky!

In the village, he traded with a farmer, seeds for diamonds.

Then he met a blacksmith with a sooty apron and a metal mask, he swapped him the axe for more diamonds.

He checked his pockets and they were empty with nothing left to trade, so he went back to his house and planted some pumpkin seeds hoping they would grow and he could use them to trade and make delicious pumpkin soup. After all, he was hungry after a long day out.

Ah, it had been a big day of play, he pressed the button on his tablet and tumbled onto his soft bed, he was back at his real home.

Putting his tablet on charge, he headed downstairs to his eat dinner and funnily enough it was pumpkin soup!

The next time Bob was sucked into the game, he saw something very unusual! When he looked outside his window there was a bunch of skeletons and zombies fighting each other for the land and trying to plant their flag posts into the ground.

Bob went outside and tried to stop them, since he didn't want a bunch of monsters near his house, but they over-powered Bob easily because there were so many of them, and only one of him.

He ran away and saw he had only one life left on his game, so he quickly pressed the button on his tablet and it took him back, tumbling again back onto his fluffy bed and grabbing his teddy.

He was happy to be home, he realized that you shouldn't try to fight an army, especially alone.

Bob played 'Block Crafting' again and this time he wanted more diamonds to trade with the nearby village.

He found a cave where he got some coal to heat up his oven.

He dug all the way under the deep earth, it was spiralled like a snails' shell, with lava in the centre and surprisingly only a few diamonds.

He quickly collected the diamonds in his large potato sack and explored further where he found some rubies and even more diamonds.

As he made his way back up, the wind was whistling peacefully, and he felt the cool breeze on his face. He arrived back at his house, noticing that the pumpkins had grown into large orange block pumpkins.

He couldn't wait to harvest them for his next yummy soup but for now he would be happy to be in his real home.

He pressed the button that would send him out of the game and again he appeared on his bed.

He headed downstairs hungry and looking forward to his dinner, which was again pumpkin soup!

But this time with roast potatoes and gravy seasoned with thyme!

After that, his tablet went back to normal and it didn't suck him into the game as it did for those four weeks.

Bob was relieved that there were no more problems with his tablet, so he could play normally again but he missed his little block house.

Daisy's New Friend
by Chloe Stevens aged 9

There once lived a small and timid little girl named Daisy. Since the day she was born, Daisy hadn't spoken a word to anyone and had never made an effort to get involved with anything. Every night she would go to sleep dreaming of the day she would make a friend, but it felt like that day would never come. Or would it?

Our story begins on a frosty, bitter day as Daisy crunched her way through the powdery snow. A cab began driving alongside her and at the sound of the revving engine she looked up from her feet to see what it was. Daisy looked through the front window of the cab and squinted to see the person inside. She couldn't see properly but whoever [or whatever] it was, she did not like them [or it] so she decided to walk the longer way to school. No sooner had she turned down the back street onto West Gate Road, than the cab was next to her again. Daisy thought she would just have to deal with the cab driving alongside her and sooner or later it would turn off at Ainslie Street. But it did not. The cab drove down Rutland Street and until the last corner of Titchfield Street. Halfway down Titchfield Street, the cab vanished into thin air.

Daisy pinched herself to check she wasn't dreaming. She definitely was not. Clutching her school satchel in one hand, Daisy rushed over to where the cab had disappeared. She examined the area with her fingers and soon discovered that there was a hole, but no ordinary hole, a teleporting hole. Curious, Daisy reached further down. A sucking sensation filled her body. She was slowly being sucked down the hole.

It was not long before Daisy appeared in a cosy little wooden shack upon a hillside.

"Hello there," said a kindly voice from behind her. Daisy spun around.

"My name is Lavender. Welcome to Friend Hill. I know all about you, Daisy." Daisy found herself warming to this woman she had barely met; it was like they had an instant bond.

"First, I must show you to your room."

And that is where Daisy slept happily for the months to come. Every day, Lavender would teach her lessons about the world and how to treat it. These lessons would often include learning magic and meeting new people. Daisy thoroughly enjoyed everything about these lessons and loved having Lavender for company. Lavender was now not just a friend. She was like a second mother to Daisy. One particular day, Lavender requested for Daisy to meet her at the wishing well.

"I have decided upon something that makes me sad," said Lavender. "I have decided it is time for you to leave my house. You have a family of your own and a life you must live. I have taught you everything you need to know. Do you agree?"

"But Lavender, I love it here!" Protested Daisy.

"That is why I wanted to bring you to this place," replied Lavender, producing a powdery substance from her satchel.

"This is fairy dust. Some was given to me when I was your age." Lavender began sprinkling the fairy dust over the wishing well and gently whispered, "hope and guidance is what I wish, for this girl to have a life full of bliss." Daisy thought it was very thoughtful of Lavender to use her only fairy dust on her and thanked Lavender gratefully afterwards. "Now, we must be heading back to the wooden shack otherwise you will never make it home." Chuckled Lavender as she took Daisy's hand. The pair scrambled back to the wooden shack, laughing and joking as they always had done. But when they got back, there was an awkward silence. Daisy sorrowfully packed her things and squeezed Lavender's hand. They shared one last hug and one last smile until Daisy left to start her own adventure. Almost immediately, she saw that haunting cab again. It pulled over beside Daisy and inside was a lobster driver! He beckoned for her to climb in, so she did as she was told. The lobster was Australian, and Daisy was still a little bit scared.

"G'day mate! What you been up to?" Asked the lobster cheerfully. Daisy was reluctant to answer but thought it would be rude if she didn't answer.

"Learning with Lavender," said Daisy miserably.

"Oooh! So, what you learnt?" replied the lobster.

"Magic, and how to make friends," answered Daisy. "Where are we going Mr Lobster?"

"Lonely Road. I heard you need a friend and there'll be plenty of people there to make friends with," responded the lobster pleasantly.

The rest of the journey was in silence until they came to a grim, grey road where lots of sad-looking people and creatures were lolloping about. "This is it. Lonely Road for ya," said the lobster.

"What? This?" replied Daisy, unimpressed.

"Yes, this. Told ya there would be loads of people to make friends with." Joked the lobster cheekily. "They weren't what I had in mind. In fact, nothing like what I had in mind. They couldn't be worse," muttered Daisy disappointedly.

"Oh well, I'll take ya somewhere else then," responded the lobster.

"Wait!" cried Daisy. "Him. Over there. That turtle."

"OK, I'll drive ya over."

And the lobster did just that. Daisy got out and strolled over to the turtle. She sat down beside him.

"Hello," she said. "My name is Daisy. What is yours?"

"Oh M – Me? My name is Tommy," replied Tommy timidly.

"Nice to meet you, Tommy. Would you like to be my friend?" asked Daisy kindly.

"Me? Oh yes I – I would be honoured!" said Tommy.

"Come with me. There's someone I think you might like to meet."

Daisy gestured as she grabbed Tommy's hand.

They got in the cab together and started a nice conversation with each other. Onwards they plodded with each other for company, and with each other to talk to. Best friends forever.

Ginger Taxi and Candy Rush
by Autumn Gristy aged 9

On a sunny Saturday two best friends called Naomi and Jack were at the recycling centre with Mrs Hawk and Giselle (Naomi's mum and sister). They were about to leave when Mrs Hawk had an emergency call from work so she said, "ok kids I have to go to a meeting at the office but I heard the amusements are open at the new leisure park. Why don't you go there for a bit?"

"Sure, but you have to give us some money" replied Naomi.

"Only 20 bucks" replied Mrs Hawk.

"Each?" asked Naomi.

"Ummm... Go on then have 20 bucks each but you do have your own card and cash you can use too." she replied back.

Mrs Hawk arranged to text them later to pick them up as she hurriedly got into her car.

The new amusement Park was a good two-mile walk from the recycling centre; it took forever to get there.

When they arrived, they had got some candy floss and three toffee apples Jack and Giselle went on the helter-skelter and other rides. Naomi wanted to save some money for later; so, she waited by the bike stand as the others went on the rides. Whilst she was waiting, she heard a weird sound come from a bush so she followed the noise finding a hole big enough that she could walk through. There was nothing there until, a dark yet spooky-looking shape started to appear.... then suddenly the noise got louder and the next thing a car came straight at her. The car was floating in the air, the wheels were moving, it suddenly stopped by the side of her. Naomi stared at the car; it was a black taxicab with a man in it.

It took him a while to see Naomi but when he did, he opened the window, it all happened in a flash!

The driver opened the car door and got out. "Good day today to you," he said, but Naomi didn't answer she just stared in silence and shock.

"Umm... Are you alright?" asked the cab driver.

"I... I'm... who are you?" Naomi stuttered.

"I'm Martin and this is Ginger." Said Martin whilst pointing to a ginger cat floating on the passenger seat. There was silence. "Ginger use your manners," Martin said. "Hi, I'm Ginger," Ginger said in a grumpy voice.

"uh well, my name... my... I mean your name is... I, uh, my name is Naomi." Naomi said in a freaked-out voice.

"Why don't you hop in and we can go somewhere... no charge of course!" Martin said. Naomi was curious about the cat who was grinning at her and she felt compelled to find out more about this floating taxi. "Sure," Naomi said in a kind of questioning way, not knowing why she was getting into the car really!

She hopped in the front and Martin made Ginger the cat get into the back. Ginger was not happy to be going in the back, he was making grumbly noises looking at Naomi. Naomi loved cats but this cat was fierce and rude.

"What singer do you like to listen to?" asked Martin.

"Um..." it took a moment for Naomi to think of one; then she stuttered, "Ariana Grande and Olly Murs are my favourite singers. "

"Ohhh I like them," said Martin.

He looked for a CD with Ariana Grande and Olly Murs music on. As Martin turned on the engine Naomi scrambled to get her seat belt on as the car floated in the air again. Naomi had forgotten about Elliot and Giselle.

"Where are we going?" Naomi asked.

Martin chuckled saying, "what about we teleport to a new world; how about candy land?" He did not wait for an answer, within seconds they were at their destination! Naomi thought to herself this is awesome.

She hopped out of the car and started drooling at all the candy, she ran over to a pile of sherbet and started eating it she wanted to know what it tasted

60

like with coke so she grabbed some and went to the river of coke and drank it.

It was a fizzy bubbling explosion in her mouth. After a while of eating everything she could see, she started having a massive sugar rush. The clouds in the sky looked like marsh mellows. The smell was amazing! Martin got out of the taxi leaving Ginger who was fast asleep.

The sun was made from a gigantic gob stopper, you just wanted to lick it! There was popping candy on the floor every few seconds popping under her feet. They were using jellybeans as bricks to make buildings it was like a film where they go to a new world and they do lots of fun things. Naomi had seen those kinds of films, but she didn't think anything like that could happen to her.

Martin started to panic as he realized the time; if you overstay your welcome you will become candy.

He grabbed Naomi desperately trying to get her back to the taxi but she just wanted more candy! She grabbed all the candy she could reach as she was dragged back to the car.

Back in the taxi ginger opened one eye and then closed it as he continued to purr, not interested in them returning. Martin took Naomi back to where he found her, he said not to tell anyone about the magic taxi so they could go on another adventure together soon.

He said all Naomi needed to do was call for a Ginger taxi and he would be there. Naomi heard the bushes move whilst Elliot and Giselle were calling her. "Where have you been?" they asked Naomi.

"Nowhere, how were the rides?" replied Naomi and she walked back through the bushes glancing back smiling with an amazing sugar taste in her mouth!

Naomi acted like nothing had happened, but she wouldn't forget about Martin and Ginger.

The Power Stones
by Maria aged 9

Hi, my name is Isabel, I live with my two sisters Nina and Katie, and my mum and dad.

I love books, coding, and cooking. Katie loves music, writing stories, and badminton. Nina loves board games, running, and art.

We live in London, but we are moving to the countryside.

This is what happened to us.

"Here's the taxi," said Mum.

"We are off! " exclaimed Nina.

We got into the taxi and then drove away, it was a long drive but, it was worth it, for the cottage was sweet, roses hung at the door and around the windows hung honeysuckle. Waiting at the door was the moving van and 2 men were moving everything in. Dad helped the men; Mum went to light the stove and make them all a cup of hot chocolate and me and my sisters carried in all the hand luggage. Then we asked Mum if we could explore and she said 'yes'.

We found a beautiful meadow covered in flowers and a fruit orchard, and we made a mental note to tell Mum about that.

Then we came to some mysterious-looking woods, the leaves shimmered in the sun like diamonds and they were a darker green than usual. We ventured into the woods and we came to a lake with stones along each side and had some fun skimming them. Then we each picked up a mysterious looking rock, they were an ordinary grey colour, but they shimmered and sparkled as if they were diamonds.

At that point, we didn't know it. but the stones were magical and we each got a magic power from our stone.

Then we skimmed them and looked up at the sky and saw it was getting late, so we went home and on the way, they chatted about what had happened and agreed not to tell our parents in case we were forbidden to go there again.

That night when we were having some warm milk before bed, I started moving my hand and the milk glass moved without me touching it, we were all confused. We thought about what had happened throughout the day, and that led us to talk about when we held the stones, we realized that the stones must have been magical. So, Nina and Katie tried moving the glass, but nothing happened, we thought that maybe we were wrong. We felt very disappointed and suddenly Nina said. "Maybe each stone gives you a different power?" We thought that this was possible so we decided that the next day we would try and find out if Nina and Katie had powers.

The next day when we had woken up, Mum made us jam and butter sandwiches for breakfast that we ate with some warm and delicious milk. Then dad sent us to clear out the back garden. I had to weed the untidy vegetable bed and my sisters had to organise the shed, we planted some flowers, as Nina had found some flower seeds while we were cleaning, but as soon as Katie watered some of the flowers they immediately grew and bloomed. We then realised that Katie's power was the power of growth. "Now we just had to find Nina's power," said Katie.

We worked hard for the rest of the day by organizing our rooms, going to the local market to get ingredients for Mum to cook, and then just like that all our work was done so we were allowed to play in the garden. We played skipping and Katie won with the most skips, then it was time for dinner, which was chicken pie, after which we went to bed. The new day had arrived and we had scrambled eggs for breakfast, Nina clapped in delight because she loved scrambled eggs and to our surprise, we saw her disappear, we told her and she stopped clapping and nothing happened, so she clapped once again and she came back we now knew that her power was invisibility.

Then Mum came in and said we could go out, so we went to the woods and explored. We came to this abandoned-looking house, we went in to see what it was like, and by the flickering candlelight, we vaguely saw someone on a glittering throne surrounded by elves that seemed to be their servants. We went to see who was on the throne and we saw a woman with golden hair that tumbled down her back, she wore a glittering crown and a sparkly blue dress. We heard an elf say her name and it was 'Emily'. We started to sneak out, but we made too much noise and Emily turned around and saw us, so all the elves started running after us, but we managed to get home safely. What we didn't know was that an elf had turned invisible and followed us home and then went to tell Emily where we live, and so she made a plot to find out if we had magic.

First, she told the elf to come back to our house and see what happened while she worked her magic.

To discover our powers, she flooded the bedroom and I managed to fix it with my power. Then she killed all the vegetables in the garden and Katie fixed it with hers. Then she put something very funny in our bedroom and Nina clapped because she thought I put it there as a joke, and she always claps when she gets excited, and she turned invisible so the elf reported all of this to Emily.

The reason she thought we had powers was because she had left the stones by the lake for safekeeping, so she knew the power of the stones.

Then Emily sent a letter to us asking us to fight a battle to see who was the most powerful, when we read this we straight away thought 'no' but then we read the small print and it said 'if you don't I will destroy your house and everything in it'. We were forced to say 'yes' so, we sent a note back saying, 'okay we will begin tomorrow'.

The next day we got set for the biggest challenge we had ever faced, we asked our parents if they could have the day free and they said 'yes' as there was no work to do.

So, we headed out to the woods to face Emily.

She was there already. "Right, let's head to the battlefield," Emily ordered, and we all walked behind her as she led the way.

As soon as we were ready and in position Emily shot a rock at us, but I used my magic to make a wave to send it back to her. She managed to duck but she got weaker and we realized that with every failed attack she grew weaker and weaker. So, Katie grew a plant monster that tore at Emily's dress and turned it to rags, then it snapped her crown. We understood that one more attack and we would win. Just as we were about to attack she sent a spiky metal ball towards us, we couldn't see a way out so we tried to run to the side, but she moved the ball to follow us, just as it was about to strike us, Nina turned us invisible so we wouldn't be seen and she couldn't use the ball to harm us.

We walked away from the ball and showed ourselves and Emily became so weak that we knew we had won. Triumphantly we left and lived a comfortable life, only using our magic for good, without the evil lady bothering us ever again.

Chaos in Space
by Matthew Jenkins aged 9

"Ben come downstairs!"

"Ok Mum," said Ben

"We're going to go on a trip," said Ben's mum.

Ben rushed down the stairs because he hadn't had his breakfast. Ben quickly ate his breakfast and brushed his teeth. He liked to brush his teeth because he had a fancy electric toothbrush.

Ben and his mum hopped into the car.

"Where are we going?" asked Ben.

Mum replied. "We're going to see your great aunt."

"Oh goodie," said Ben.

Ben liked their car because they got it last month. It had four comfy seats, it had a built-in tv, and a mini-fridge with Ben's favourite drink inside which was Coke Zero.

This drink reminded him of Spain, so he loved his car.

While he was in the car, he got bored and said, "Mum, can I get out the I-pad?"

His mum replied saying he could have it for a little while.

Ben's mum did not like Ben playing on screens too much because Ben's mum had read that you should only play for 1 hour a day in a news article last Wednesday.

So, when Ben had finished using his I-pad he saw a road going to a petrol station.

Ben said, "Mum we should go and get some petrol!"

Ben and his mum went down the lane and then they saw a magic looking yellow taxi. Ben asked his mum if they could take some time out of their journey to take a look at the taxi?

"Sure," said Ben's mum.

When he got in the taxi it felt bigger than it really was, and you could not see the taxi driver through the glass. The taxi started to move, and Ben and his mum felt a little curious and worried.

Ben's mum said, "I am sure we will be fine." But then his mum looked out of the window, she said. "WE'RE IN OUTER SPACE AND WE'RE HEADING FOR A FLOATING BUILDING!"

When they got out of the taxi, they were greeted by a staff member at the front of the building and he said, "Welcome, sorry about that ride it must have been a bit bumpy."

"Yes, it was, "said Ben's mum still in shock.

The staff member smiled. "You will stay the night, we have a pool, football pitch, and 3,000 rooms with a mini-fridge especially for you."

"Coke Zero for me please," said Ben.

"Good," said the staff member, "you are in room 290 and 291." As he said this he handed over the keys.

"Thanks," said Ben and his mum.

"Oh, and don't use the stairs it will take too long, use the lift instead."

When Ben and his mum got to their rooms, they were astonished- it was luxurious!

There was a leaflet that explained all they wanted to know about the place they were staying.

'This hotel in space has 2 large engines that are powered by rocket fuel but hopefully one day it will be powered by solar panels."

When they were having dinner, the main engine went down so for the next hour they had to stay in their room. Ben was a little scared, he decided to go and help. He went to the Captain's office. The Captain was sleeping so Ben woke him up.

"Wake up!" said Ben.

"You… you what?" said the Captain.

Ben said. "The engine is down."

"WHAT?" said the Captain. "I'll get my men to figure out what is going on!"

"Thanks, "said Ben.

"That's alright," said the captain. "My men should fix it soon."

"Good," said Ben.

"Bye."

When Ben was going back to his room, he heard a whispered voice saying, "yes, we should really shut down the magic taxi cab service."

Ben rushed to the manager and said, "I overheard a plot to shut down the magic taxi cab service."

The manager replied, "don't be silly!"

Ben knew that nobody would listen to him because he was only a child and the manager was too busy. The manager needed to go to a meeting on the computer with world leaders with prime ministers and presidents. They wanted to discuss the launch of the space hotel. Yes, launch! Ben and his mum had early access! It turns out they were the first-ever guests at the space hotel!

Ben ran down the stairs as fast as a cheetah, he saw what was wrong with the engine.

He tried to fix it, but it was no good. Then he saw a toolbox, he ran over to the toolbox and then heard a worker's voice saying, "oh I heard that the engine went down Lewis and I think we need to fix it."

Ben dashed into the shadows and hid. He waited, perched on the shelving unit. Finally, the coast was clear, and he got the toolbox and went over to the engine, it still wasn't fixed.

"Ah," said Ben. Ben tried and tried to fix the engine and then he saw that there was a fuel leak. "Oh no," said Ben he had no clue what to do.

Ben whooshed back up to the Captain's office and breathlessly shouted to the Captain. "FUEL LEAK."

The Captain jumped out of his seat and rushed down the stairs and took a look at the fuel leak.

Thankfully, he knew what to do. He got all of his workers to fix it and they successfully completed the job, but then the taxi service went down.

Ben felt awful and was worried that he and his mum might never get back home. The plot Ben had overheard earlier about getting rid of the magic taxi service must have worked but just then the computer they were running the hack on had a battery malfunction and the plot failed. The taxi was working again.

Then Ben and his mum went back on the bumpy taxi ride and had an awesome day with their great aunt.

The Crazy Trip
by Phoebe Golledge aged 9

One bright morning, three small animals were packing up their bags. "I am going to take the bouncy castle that has a humongous rainbow on it," said Bonga the bunny.

"Ok Bonga," replied Steve the squirrel. Steve's brother Calum the chipmunk is very shy, so he talks very quietly and high-pitched. Once they had finished packing, they made breakfast. "What's for breakfast today Bonga?" asked Calum shyly.

"Well Calum you will be happy to know that I am making you sizzle pop bang," said Bonga in her usual jolly voice.

Sizzle pop bang is a delicious cereal that when you eat it you feel your tummy go sizzle pop bang. "Mmmmmm," hummed Calum as he enjoyed the food.

Sometime later, they had finished eating and it was all hands on deck to clear up. They made quite a lot of mess eating, especially Steve because he always likes to be the first one to finish. Bonga put the rubbish away and cleared the table. Calum washed up and Steve dried everything. They had a couple more jobs and then they were ready to leave.

RING, RING, went the phone. "Hello, it is Tilly the tortoise from Taxi World. I am just checking you want a pick up at 9 am?" said Tilly in her work voice.

"Oh, hello Tilly can we change the time to half 8 instead because we are ready now?" asked Bonga.

"Sure you can. I'm on my way," replied Tilly. A few minutes later, Tilly arrived to pick up the friends. They were all sitting in the back of the lemon yellow taxi cab. "Would you like some music?" asked Tilly

"Oooh, yes, please. Can we have the album 'Sing it like it Rocks'?" asked Steve because that was his favourite.

"Sure," said Tilly putting the album on.

The destination for the three friends was Treetops Village, a hotel complex with many on-site activities including water skiing, a sculpture trail, and an enormous zip wire from tree to tree. The drive to Treetops is about 2 hours. On the way, they went past the church, the schools, the food shops, the shopping centre, the cinema, and theatre. As they went past the Animal Theme Park suddenly, they heard a loud sizzle pop bang! The friends found themselves not in the lemon yellow taxi cab but instead on a Jungle Rollercoaster.

The carriage went all the way to the top of the rollercoaster. Then down the steep drop surrounded by a cascading waterfall. Round the loopy loop landing in the parkour course. Next, it travelled across the monkey swinging vines, under the dinosaur legs, then through a cavernous tunnel.

"Aaaaaaaaa!" Screamed everyone. "This is an epic ride!" said Calum. Then quick as a flash, they were back in the taxi.

"Whoa, what happened there?" spluttered Steve.

The journey continued calmly, just as they were about to doze off SIZZLE POP BANG! This time they were in a fabulous food market featuring produce from all over the world. They whizzed around the market and feasted on carrots, peas, cake, donuts, and pizza amongst other things. Then once again, they were back in the taxi cab.

"This is super weird," stated Bonga the bunny.

"I wonder if there is something magical about our cereal? Haven't you guys noticed we keep hearing sizzle pop bang right before we are magically transported somewhere?"

Calum and Steve said in unison, "oh yeah you are right."

"I am intrigued to know where we will end up next," pondered Calum. No sooner had he spoken these words when Sizzle Pop Bang they were off again!

The location this time was the zoo. They went past sleeping lions and fierce tigers and relaxed bears and munching giraffes. They saw hungry penguins being fed and muddy rhinos having a bath. After that they saw a dolphin show; the dolphins jumped high into the sky. They visited a large group of pandas tucking into a breakfast of bamboo. Lastly, they went into the aquarium where they saw an amazing collection of different types of fish. "I love the aquarium!" said Bonga.

Sitting again in the back seat of the taxi cab the three friends caught their breath.

"Tilly how long left until this crazy trip is over?" asked Calum. "It will be about 10 minutes until we arrive at Treetops, where the tallest trees are," replied Tilly.

"I can't take much more of this, please no more sizzle pop bang!" pleaded Steve.

"We've arrived!" shouted Tilly pulling up at the Treetops hotel. What they saw was a series of treetop houses placed in between thick oak trees. Each house had a large wide balcony looking out onto a shimmering lake. Each front door was a different colour, and all were named after trees.

Tilly unloaded their bags and as she walked over to them to say goodbye, the friends asked her. "Does this usually happen when you drive your taxi cab?" Tilly replied, "does what happen?"

"Every time we heard sizzle pop bang we disappeared off to a different place for a magical adventure. We went to a theme park, a market, and a zoo!" explained Calum.

"I have not a clue what you are talking about. It was one of my most peaceful journeys, in fact, you were asleep the whole time," said Tilly in surprise.

The friends looked at each other with their mouths wide open in amazement. "There is definitely something magical about that cereal."

Laughed Steve and the three of them went off to start their next exciting adventure.

The End

The Mystery of The Three-Headed Creature
by Adam Seymour aged 9

Chapter 1

Harry Lasfor lived with his older sister Poppy, his younger brother Matt and his parents Bob and Jemima. His dad was a taxi driver and his mum worked as a police officer for the local police station. Poppy was in Year 7 and Matt Year 1, while Harry was in Year 5. They were very happy in their small cottage located in a remote seaside town in Devon.

Every night, they would eat dinner and their father would tell them about his day and some of the funny, stupid and posh passengers he met, as well as many others. After that, it would be their mother's turn.

On that particular Tuesday evening, Bob had just told them about his passengers; one of them an angry man who gave him the wrong directions and was late for a wedding; another who took the mickey out of him for the whole journey and several others that he had interesting conversations with. Now it was Jemima's turn. First, she told them about someone escaping, then about some weird dolls that had been handed in, and finally about some witnesses seeing a three-headed man of some sort stealing jewellery and food.

That night, Harry went to bed thinking about that three-headed-man, could it be an alien, that his mum had talked about? Stealing things people loved. "How horrible," he whispered, "it must leave people feeling tormented." Then he clutched his teddy bear and drifted sound asleep. "Night." he murmured to his mum.

"Night!" she called back

At school the next day, Harry found out even more about the creature.

Jose's Uncle was a newspaper writer for the Sleek Black Cats Newspaper, and he had written about something that involved a terrifying monster with six oddly shaped ears. "Whoa, that's WICKED!!!" exclaimed Liddy excitedly. "It's scary AND dangerous!" replied Michael, the smartest and most sensible kid in school. Most kids thought he was an idiot, but Harry thought he was a cool nerd.

The next morning, he ate breakfast and at school he heard a rumour of a creature with bloodshot eyes, four noses, and a perfect jet-black Mohawk perched neatly on its head.

That night, when Harry's dad told his story, Harry knew something was up. The description that Bob gave to his family was of a tall man with massive, broad shoulders, eyes oddly to one side and pink skin like Peppa Pig (embarrassingly, a favourite programme of his). After his mum had said more witnesses had reported the anonymous creature, Harry Lasfor's mind was buzzing with so many questions straining tirelessly to get out.

Chapter 2

On that cold Thursday morning, Harry came up with a plan. With the help of his three best friends - Ryan, Jose, and Liz - he was going to try and find out who this strange creature or alien was and hopefully get a reward (although that wasn't the main reason he was doing it).

What Harry didn't know was that the witnesses were mistaken, and the alien thingy was innocent.

As soon as Harry got into school, he tried to tell them about his plan, but the bell rang before he had time. During maths, Harry tried the strategy of sending messages through paper aeroplanes, but they had Miss Claroon as a substitute teacher who was very nosey, so that didn't work.

After a boring maths lesson, in which they learned long multiplication, it was break time and that meant Harry finally had an opportunity to tell them the plan. Before he could share any of his plan, he remembered something. "Oh no!" Harry shouted a bit too loudly when he suddenly realised, "I entered myself in the football competition!"

"What is wrong with you?!" exclaimed Mrs Narang, the snappy Year 5 teacher, "keep your horrible voice down!"

After playing in a football match, which his team won 4-1, (Harry scoring a hat-trick) his class piled inside the warm classroom.

"I'll let you know at lunch," he promised his friends. After a fun English lesson, they went outside. Harry was feeling victorious until he realised, he had extra science lessons with Professor Macklewen.

This time he didn't shout but cursed under his breath. Luckily, no one heard otherwise he'd have been in big trouble! After a very messy science lesson with Professor Macklewen, his coat had a couple of stains on it and that meant one thing: ANGRY MUM!!!!!

After geography and history, Harry had the perfect opportunity to tell them about his plan. He described the pink-faced creature with four noses and three heads.

"The immense shoulders must have been the robber's two other heads on either side tucked up in its disguise. And let me tell you the plan!" Harry exclaimed.

"You're a genius!" remarked Ryan after he had finished. "Well done!"

"Thanks!" replied Harry happily, "do you want to be part of the adventure?"

"YES!!!" they all screamed loudly. So loudly, in fact, a cow all the way in Mexico heard them.

Chapter 3

Harry went to bed excited that his friends knew his plans.

His mum hadn't been too angry about the coat, but she and his father had let Poppy talk during dinner as it was her first school trip today. Harry didn't mind, he already knew lots about the monster. The plan was that they would all ask their parents more about it and collect the information and then finally capture the three-headed weirdo (and hopefully get a prize).

Thankfully, the next day, Harry didn't have a football match or any extra lessons, so they all poured out their information. Liz's Auntie's friend had been robbed by what she claimed to be a four-nosed evil creature.

Ryan's mum also wrote for The Sleek Black Cats Newspaper and someone had seen a 'horrible creature' chasing after a thick, bulky man in jet black jeans and a matching bullet-proof jacket.

On a very normal Friday night, Harry's father had been casually talking about his passengers and then something happened that turned it into a very abnormal night.

"Right" their mother had said, "your Aunt Peggy has been robbed by a man with sharp studs all over his body."

"Oh no!" whispered Matt to Harry, "Aunt Peggy smells of cat sick."

"And," she continued loudly and sternly over Matt, "the man was chased away by a strange creature who saved her. We must be cautious, okay children?"

"Yes, mother!" They all said together.

On the way to school, Harry saw a three-headed alien stopping a bad looking man wearing a bullet-proof jacket and returning a wad of stolen cash to a terrified old woman!

The police were informed that the alien was innocent, and the man was caught and went to prison.

A Mystical Spell
by Amisha K. Davies aged 10

I drove around the lush countryside, cool air flying through my window.

I worked in a taxi company.

I wasn't working at the moment. I just loved the countryside and the sights - tall mountains, cloaked in early morning mist, the chirrup of wrens, and kingfishers.

I drove slowly, taking in all the sights, gazing out to see splashing, sapphire rivers and the lime coloured hills. I drove around here often. It was a place for me to think and separate myself from any worries or problems.

The towering trees swayed gently in the swift breeze, and the falling leaves created a jumble of colours in neatly stacked mounds.

As I drove, I noticed something in the far distance. It was a bit blurred since I was a long way away, but I made something out that was shaped like a tunnel, although there was no train track, and no way for any cars to reach there.

I parked up, opened my door, and stepped out then I ran and ran towards the strange tunnel.

Even after a few minutes, I was dripping with perspiration, although I realised that I'd nearly made it there. I steadied myself into a slow walk as I neared.

Closer now, I could see that it wasn't a tunnel. But a cave entrance. I approached with careful steps and cautiously crept inside.

The walls were caked in mud, and I could decipher an orange and peach shade on them.

I'd been so absorbed in glaring at the entrance, I didn't notice what was actually inside.

There was a marble stand, brave and proud in the dark of the cave. Placed with care on the top, was a dusty, old book.

I was fixated and drew closer. Imprinted on the open pages, was the phrase; 'Those who read will be provided an opportunity that they would never have got'.

Puzzled, I wondered what it meant.

It had been left lying open on the first two pages and so I flicked carefully through the rest of the book.

All the words were in English, and I could read them easily.

And I did. Aloud.

"This mystical creature with two wings, can do a few magical things," I read. A swirl of smoke emanated throughout the space. The smoke cleared and I saw a shape, it resembled a green dragon with scaly skin and golden wings. I blinked in disbelief. I wondered if it could speak English since it had come out of a book.

"Hello," I said in a cheery voice.

It just looked at me confused.

"What are the chances?" I muttered under my breath. "I must be seeing things. It's my mind playing tricks on me," I spun round to head back outside.

"I think I can speak English. I just haven't given it a go since I've been stuck in that book," the dragon said. He had a low, gruff voice, perfectly fitting for a dragon.

"So . . . so you can speak?" I said, raising my eyebrows. I was acting as if this wasn't much.

"It seems I can speak English! As you've freed me, would you mind awfully getting my friends out by reading the spells?" He inquired politely.

"We've been trapped in that book for centuries and no-one's freed us since . . . Well, forever."

"OK. It can't do much harm then," I said, bluntly.

"Thank you!" the dragon cried. "Thank you ever so much!"

"No problem."

I reached for the book once again and read out the next spell.

"I can fly, soar up in the sky, have a shining horn, my oh my," I read slowly. In another puff of smoke, a white unicorn, spotty with shiny stars and a rainbow horn stood behind me.

"It's great to be out!" the unicorn said. "Thank you," she added as she turned to me.

"It's fine," I said.

"Would you mind freeing our pixie friend?" the dragon asked. "That's all we want."

"Yeah, of course," I said shooting a smile to both of them in turn.

"She has see-through wings and small in size, the best creature, and no-one can despise."

A pixie materialized in front of me.

She skipped through any greetings and showered me in thanks.

"It's fine," I repeated. "Hey, unicorn!" I said. "Do you ever give anyone any rides?"

"I'd love to give it a go," she said.

Before she could say a word more, I hopped onto her back.

"Hold on tight!" she called out.

She lowered herself as we glided through the cave entrance. Immediately after, she went straight up and straight down as quick as a peregrine falcon. Halfway down, she lifted up and soared through the sky, passing through clouds as high as planes and hot air balloons. The air lit my face up and I felt the adrenaline as this once-in-a-lifetime opportunity was all mine.

She soared over tall peaks, rocky cliff faces, and every should-see scenery that there was.

She landed gracefully back at the cave entrance.

As I unmounted I realised that the dragon was bigger and had greater wings, that would have been a quicker ride, but no use complaining.

"Thanks," I said. It was my turn to say that word. "Where did the spellbook come from anyway?" I enquired.

The dragon's face darkened.

"A long time ago," he began, "there was an evil Wizard. He'd hunted us down for fame and glory. He had caught us, but we managed to escape, then he put a spell on this book," the dragon indicated the spellbook. "He caught us inside it and put a spell on us so we would be trapped until someone said the magic words to free us."

"Me then?" I pointed at myself.

"Yes, you," the pixie said.

"Great chatting to you, but you're going to have to go."

"Go? Go where?" the unicorn asked.

"Back in the book. You can't roam about," I said.

"Can't we?" the dragon questioned "Please."

"OK. But as long as you stay in the countryside."

"Thank you!" the pixie cried.

I left them in a bundle of happiness.

And that's where they still are. If you drive around the countryside and look closely, you might, maybe, see one of them if you keep your eyes peeled.

I hopped into my taxi and waved goodbye – although it might not be the last meeting I had with my new friends.

Enchanted Talking Taxi
by Alannah Batteux aged 12

"Cars for sale! Good deals! Low prices!" The salesman hollered with all his might, but the busy crowd ignored him.

"Yes! Sir, do you have any taxi cabs?" Timothy ran towards the man. His taxi had unfortunately broken down only the day before, and he needed a new one.

"We sure do! Come, follow me." The man gestured for Timothy to follow him. "Here are some, brand new ones! I'll give you time to choose."

"Oh, no need! You see, I need this taxi today, I'll pick very quickly."

Timothy quickly chose a taxi and was ready to buy it. It was brand new, the sort that is so shiny and smells fresh.

A few hours later, Timothy was very pleased with the purchase he had made, in fact, he could no longer wait and hopped into his newly bought vehicle for a drive. This made him even happier.

As he was driving, he heard a sudden noise, and what happened afterwards is crazy.

This is what happened: after the noise, the taxi seemed to have gone crazy! It somehow began to drive itself. Next thing Timothy knew was that he was no longer in the smelly busy city of
New York but in a sand dessert!

"I'm very sorry sir, I had to stretch a little," said a voice. Now Timothy was very confused.

"Who was that?! Who spoke?!" he looked around and suddenly there was no taxi, but instead, there was a boy. Then the boy spoke.

"Well it was me of course!" the boy, who looked about twelve, said.

"Who are you?! Where is my taxi? Where am I?" Timothy was frightened and yet so confused.

"Don't be so scared! My name's Jack." Timothy was still confused, "I'm the taxi, you know... the one you bought, yes, I know I'm a human right now but I'm a taxi, and yes, I talk!" Timothy stared, mouth wide open. How was this possible... the taxi cab he bought... was a human??!

"Sorry I- I don't-? How... where is- taxi? Who- what-?" Timothy exclaimed, it is normal to be lost for words when something so unexplainable happens, especially when it is something you can't understand. Poor Timothy was bewildered.

"I'm sorry." Said Jack. "I know you don't see this every day. Let me explain... It's a long story so I'll give you the short version. You see me right now, as a boy, that's what I am. When I was younger, I was left in front of a professor's home, he took me in and looked after me. One day a man turned up who claimed to be my father, turns out he was just a very evil magician. He cast a spell on the professor who had looked after me. And he enchanted me too, since I was 5, I have been enchanted by a spell that makes me a taxi. Yes, I know it's a weird story. It's hard to explain because nowadays no one believes in magic anymore, but it exists or at least it used to. My enchantment can never be broken, it's my fate" Jack looked down, upset.

"Oh, wow!" Timothy was now no longer confused but shocked. "I'm sorry, I wish you could be a normal boy again."

"It's alright, but I also wish I could be normal again... Can we be friends?" Jack, the taxi, asked hopefully.

"Of course! Can I ask, why can't the spell be broken?"

"I suspect the man who did this to me is very powerful, his magic must be horrible. And I'm not sure anyone in this world today can save me from the spell and go against this man."

"What about that professor, where is he?"

"I haven't seen him in a long time, but it would be no use, he too is enchanted, but it's worse for him I am sure, but I don't know where he is." Jack said.

"Oh, well if it's possible I'd like to find him and somehow break this spell."

"Yes, me too, but it's going to be very hard, I'm not sure it can be done."

"We shall try!" Timothy said with excitement.

"Yes, we shall." And as Jack said this, a great storm came and abruptly, lightning struck.

At first, it was far away but it got closer. Small fires began and thunder could be heard coming over the hills.

It wasn't a bad storm really, well at this moment it wasn't.

"Can you turn back into a taxi or whatever? We should get home quickly, looks like this is going to be a heavy storm!" Timothy quickly suggested.

"Yes! Good idea!" as he said this Jack turned into a taxi again, quite a sight to see, a boy becoming a taxi. Timothy jumped in and let Jack drive himself towards home.

Out of nowhere, lighting struck the taxi. Boom! Bang! The taxi cab crashed into a tree, slightly on fire.

It took a while for anything else to happen, Jack was... well who knows? He was hurt for sure and Timothy was unconscious, his head was hurt and bleeding. A horrible half an hour later, Timothy finally awoke and felt dreadfully bad. He got out and nearly fell because of all the sudden pain.

"Jack? Jack? My friend, are you okay?" Timothy's croaky voice seemed no use because Jack didn't answer.

After some time had passed Jack became a boy again and Timothy could now see he had been hurt in the head and leg.

"Jack?!" he spoke but got no answer.

Then...

"Ye, Timothy- is that... is that you?" Finally, Jack was waking up.

"Jack?! You're alive, this is amazing!!!"

"Yes, I'm alive! Are you okay, is your injury bad?" Jack sat up slowly and looked concerned at Timothy's bleeding.

"Oh, I'm fine, we are both okay, wow this was a day wasn't it?!"

"Yes, it definitely was, Timothy, we should really get back to town and maybe go to the emergency room!" He said.

"Yes, that would probably be best, I'm glad to have met you. You're not exactly... well, a normal human being, but you are a fun kid!"

"Yes, I am glad to have met you, you're a fun adult!" Jack the taxi, and Timothy the driver went home afterwards.

After this, the two became close.

Timothy ended up adopting Jack.

Both son and father, taxi and driver, lived happily. Then together they found the professor and the enchantment ended.

Jack was a normal boy again with a new family, but Timothy will always call him, 'Taxi Boy.'

The End.

Puddles and the Magic Taxi
by Hannah Jones aged 9

Once upon a time, there was a little penguin called Puddles.
He lived in London Zoo. One day he went for walk and got lost and he couldn't find his way home.
He called for help, but nobody came. It got dark and Puddles was hungry. Just then a big sparkly taxi came out of the sky. It stopped in front of him, so he jumped in.
The taxi started to move and soon it was going really fast across the snow. Suddenly the taxi started to fly. It flew over mountains and trees and rivers and lakes and then over a big scary jungle. And then disaster struck, the taxi ran out of magic. It crashed into the ground.
Puddles got out of the taxi. He was scared, it was night and he was tired. He fell asleep on the jungle floor.
In the morning he woke up and remembered everything. He started to cry.
"What is wrong?" said a voice. Puddles looked up. He saw a monkey at the top of a tree.
"I got lost," said Puddles. "And a flying taxi picked me up, but it ran out of magic and crashed."
"I can help you," said the monkey. "If you go far away you will find a genie. You need to go north, and it will be hard."
With that, the monkey was gone.
So, Puddles went to find the genie. He walked for a long time and then he stopped, he had come to a swamp. Then, he saw a crocodile. There was nothing to do but jump across, but he could not do that because he was too short. Then he had a crazy idea. He knew that penguins didn't fly but if he tried really hard, he might be able to do it. He ran and started to flap and flew higher and higher. But Puddles couldn't keep flying and he started to fall. The crocodiles opened their mouths ready to eat him up.

Puddles closed his eyes.

Just then he felt something lift him up into the sky. It was a parrot.

"Thank you for saving me," he said.

"You're most welcome," said the parrot. "Do you want to see the genie?"

"Yes, I do," Puddles said. "Do you know the way to the genie?"

"Of course, I know, I live here," said the parrot.

After about ten minutes the parrot landed and said, "Here you are. Goodbye."

And with that, the parrot disappeared. Puddles saw a big pearl palace with guards on each side. "Can I see the genie?" he asked.

"You can see him quickly," said one of the guards.

So, Puddles went through the big gates to find the genie. When he went inside of the big palace and he saw a person sitting on a chair.

"Can you help me find the genie please?" asked Puddles.

"I am the genie," the person said.

"Please can I have a wish?" asked Puddles.

"No," said the genie.

"Please," said Puddles. "Just one, I will do anything."

"You can have one wish if you can find the missing gold that's been missing for years and years," said the genie.

Puddles went out of the palace.

It was very hard to find missing gold, he looked everywhere but all he found was an old chest. He went back to the genie.

"All I found is this," said Puddles and showed the genie the old chest.

"You found it!" said the genie. "That chest has the gold inside."

The genie gave Puddles a lamp

"Rub this lamp and make a wish," said the genie. "I wish the magic taxi would come back," said Puddles.

"It will have more magic now and you can go home."

Puddles went back the way he had come. On the way, he found a big hole. He hadn't seen this on the way to the genie probably because he had been flying.

He did not know what to do. Just then he had an idea. He would make a bridge. He found lots of logs and sticks and made a very good bridge. Then he came back to the crocodiles. He called for the parrot, but he didn't come. There was a way Puddles could think of - to use the crocodiles as stepping-stones and he did not want to do that at all.

In the end, he had to do it. Each crocodile snapped at him, but he made it. He was very happy now, soon he would be back home at London Zoo, but he would be sad. He would miss all the friends he had made, monkey, parrot, and the genie.

"Nice to see you again," said the monkey.

"Hello," said Puddles. Then he had an idea. "How would you like to come home with me?"

"I would like to," said the monkey. "But I would miss my friends, the parrot, and the genie."

"They could come too," said Puddles.

"That's a great idea," said the monkey.

"I will have to go and tell them," said Puddles.

"You will not have to tell us," said a voice.

"Parrot you came," said Puddles. "And genie. Let's get into the magic taxi and go to London Zoo together."

They soon found the magic taxi, got in, and started moving.

"Wow I did not know it flew," said the monkey.

"This taxi can do anything," said Puddles.

But it was such a long way to the zoo, the taxi ran out of magic again.

"Oh no," said the parrot. "It has run out of magic and it is crashing."

"Don't worry," said the genie. "I wish it to be full of magic."

They got back to the zoo and they all lived happily ever after.

Dystopia
by Catherine Katesmark aged 12

POV: You get in the backseat of a taxi with a slightly-too-chatty driver...

The man stayed facing forward, but the flickering lights of the highway lit up the frown lines etched onto his face. He drummed his fingers on the steering wheel, evidently struggling with himself.
"I'm not really supposed to be telling you this. Well, I'm not supposed to be telling anyone this at all. It's highly censored government information, but I can't live with the secret any longer. Are you prepared?"
I was about to just shrug it off and simply mumble 'yes', but something in his face, reflected in the wing-mirror, made me pause.
"Yes. Sir, I'm sure no matter how ground-breaking or confidential this information might be, I can handle it."
The cabbie grunted. "Hmm. Wouldn't be too sure... but here we go."

He cleared his throat.
"Okay, well... I work undercover for a global company called... well, it doesn't really have a name, but I call it "Tectonic" taxis. We – that is, us cab drivers – move all the countries further apart, causing the earth to rupture, for a secret superpower government scheme to separate as many nations as possible from each other. Literally, to tow the world apart. A little 'nudge' from our bumpers and Africa slowly, imperceptibly, drifts further from Europe, whilst countries within continents start to fragment. Then each country will have to rely solely on their own natural resources, not borrow, or some might say "steal" from others. These governments intend to keep the strongest countries and destroy the weaker ones, to create a more 'perfect' Earth.

So, yes. To sum up in a few words, your entire life has been built on a lie. No 'tectonic plates'. No more 'migrants crossing borders'. No 'world peace'. Isolation. Just us taxi drivers, slowly moving the lands apart. It is all a big conspiracy; set up to kill millions of innocent people living in weaker areas. I don't like it one bit, haven't been able to get a good night's sleep since I was forced to sign up."

He sighs. "And the worst of it is, I can never leave."

I was unable to believe what I was hearing. A worldwide government scheme? Destroying countries? Was he really telling me all this? I couldn't believe it. But again, something in the man's voice stopped me. Was it… regret? I needed to know.

I decided to play along. "Why can you never leave? How can a taxi carry a whole country? Why do these governments think a stronger world is a world with half its countries missing?"

"Easy on the questions. I'm not supposed to be telling you this at all, remember?"

We stop at a red light and he eyes me in the mirror again.

"I can never leave because the governments don't want me to rebel against them. They've made it very clear we'll pay a fatal price. If we cabbies all left, we could form a society exposing them, and we could bring them down. So, once you're in, you're in for life. To answer your second question, we call them 'taxis' because they do the work of a taxi. But they're massive, 400 times the size of this one, and they're actually water-powered, because we need to dive deep under the oceans to separate the chunks of land. Yet another lie – sea levels aren't rising… they're falling, due to the amount of water these taxis use. A country can weigh over 3 gigatons – and these taxis can carry them easily.

My most recent job was Madagascar, and I moved it maybe a few centimetres per week. It varies, I suppose, depending on the size of the country. We get paid a huge sum of money, but we all have to get regular jobs as well, which is why I'm your taxi driver right now, because it might seem suspicious that an "unemployed man" is so rich. But if you are lazy, perhaps don't do your job properly, then 'The Boss' is who you'll have to face. And, believe me, that isn't someone you want to meet. The Boss's real name is classified; we all just say, "The Boss". I have never met 'The Boss' and I hope I never have to. I have heard rumours that they are an evil monster, a thug and all of this was their idea. I don't know why they imagine a stronger world is a world 'apart'. I mean, it's not as though we're in competition with any other planets. My brain says we ought to unite, not separate!"

He shakes his head.

"But who would listen to me?"

I was in shock. My face must have been a picture. Just as I was about to open my mouth, the taxi came to an abrupt halt. And finally, the man turned around to face me. He looked around thirty, but his shoulders slumped as though he had the weight of the world on his shoulders.

Which I suppose he did.

"£19.50, please. Oh and –" he leaned forward. "Not a word, understand? I just needed someone to talk to."

With that he snatched the money I was offering and withdrew. Without a word, I stumbled out and watched as the car drew away silently, swallowed by the night.

I turned towards my house, key in hand, and smiled softly to myself.

Silly man. I couldn't quite believe he had such little regard for his contract. I reached into my pocket and drew out a small white card. It slipped through my fingers as I moved towards my house, but I didn't need to pick it up I had plenty more. It landed gently on the wet pavement. The water had already begun to seep through the fibres, but the writing was still visible.

A. LYONS
T-T MANAGEMENT DIRECTOR

And underneath, in smaller print…

THE BOSS

My most recent job was Madagascar, and I moved it maybe a few centimetres per week. It varies, I suppose, depending on the size of the country. We get paid a huge sum of money, but we all have to get regular jobs as well, which is why I'm your taxi driver right now, because it might seem suspicious that an "unemployed man" is so rich. But if you are lazy, perhaps don't do your job properly, then 'The Boss' is who you'll have to face. And, believe me, that isn't someone you want to meet. The Boss's real name is classified; we all just say, "The Boss". I have never met 'The Boss' and I hope I never have to. I have heard rumours that they are an evil monster, a thug and all of this was their idea. I don't know why they imagine a stronger world is a world 'apart'. I mean, it's not as though we're in competition with any other planets. My brain says we ought to unite, not separate!"

He shakes his head.

"But who would listen to me?"

I was in shock. My face must have been a picture. Just as I was about to open my mouth, the taxi came to an abrupt halt. And finally, the man turned around to face me. He looked around thirty, but his shoulders slumped as though he had the weight of the world on his shoulders.

Which I suppose he did.

"£19.50, please. Oh and —" he leaned forward. "Not a word, understand? I just needed someone to talk to."

With that he snatched the money I was offering and withdrew. Without a word, I stumbled out and watched as the car drew away silently, swallowed by the night.

I turned towards my house, key in hand, and smiled softly to myself.

Silly man. I couldn't quite believe he had such little regard for his contract. I reached into my pocket and drew out a small white card. It slipped through my fingers as I moved towards my house, but I didn't need to pick it up I had plenty more. It landed gently on the wet pavement. The water had already begun to seep through the fibres, but the writing was still visible.

A. LYONS
T-T MANAGEMENT DIRECTOR

And underneath, in smaller print…

THE BOSS

The Haircut
by Tilly O'Shea aged 9

"Timothy! It's time to get your hair cut! That awful video game is being banned! Get into some nice clothes." yelled Mum.

Timothy quickly pulled on some jeans and a blue shirt and tied his hair into a small ponytail. "Ah, that's better, now get in the taxi," said Mum.

"Hi, my name is Albie your Mum's old college friend and your faithful taxi driver." exclaimed the very British driver.

"I'm Tim," he mumbled. Mum jumped in and slammed the door.

"Off we go then!" announced Albie.

They drove down the long, narrow streets of New York.

"STOP! The mall has a sale on!" Shouted Mum.

Albie swerved to a halt and let Mum hop out. "Albie as my loyal college friend would you please take Timothy to the hairdressers?" begged Mum.

"Of course." grinned Albie.

"Tim, I'll be back in three hours," said Mum. She blew a kiss back to Tim as she ran towards the mall.

"Okay Tim, we are now going on an adventure!" cried Albie.

"A haircut isn't that exciting," mumbled Tim.

"No, not the hairdressers I mean a real adventure! You'll see. Buckle up." said Albie excitedly. The weird taxi driver then pulled a key the size of a puppy out of his bag and put it into the lock of a cabinet Tim hadn't noticed before. After he unlocked it Albie revealed a selection of two buttons, one red one blue. He clicked both at the same time and suddenly they were driving down what seemed to be a completely different road...

A long yellow stone road lay ahead of them. Trees of different colours and sizes seemed to be waving at Tim, so he nervously waved back. As Tim stuck his head out the window, he couldn't believe his eyes. Winged horses spread out like butterflies, soaring across the sky their beautiful manes flying behind them glowing in the afternoon sun. Fauns were galloping on blue grass while some stopped to admire the pretty, colourful flowers. Then all types of mythical creatures were skipping about the road.

After driving down the road for ten minutes, Albie stopped driving and said, "Come on."

Tim hopped out of the car and followed Albie to a grassy clearing. "Jack, Amy!" called Albie. Then something amazing happened. A boy, the age of Tim, came down on a huge dark blue dragon. Its huge wings spread out and a silver spike sat on its nose.

Then, on a winged horse, a girl maybe a month or two younger than Tim came soaring down and jumped over the dragon. "Hi, I'm Tim," said Tim.

"Amy," the girl replied.

"I'm Jack!" said the boy.

Albie clambered onto the dragon and stretched out a hand for Tim. Tim shut his eyes and took Albie's hand. Now Albie, Tim, Jack, and Amy were flying in the mythical world on a dragon. Tim saw Amy sat on the dragon's nose, so he moved to join her.

"Nice dragon you've got," said Tim.

"Yeah, her name is Storm."

The dragon blew a fiery lightning bolt at the mention of her name.

Tim gazed at Amy but then got so distracted he slipped off the dragon, Jack caught him just in time but lost his footing and slipped off instead.

"AAAAAAGH!" yelled Jack. "

You just killed my brother! You idiot!" Amy yelled so loud it echoed.

Amy looked down, watching hopefully for any sign that her brother was ok. Tim nervously clambered back to Albie and asked him, "What are we doing here?"

"We have to save this magnificent world. If you look down here, everything is dark and ruined and that is going to happen everywhere and to everyone who lives here if we don't find the fountain of Potenza Blu. That's Italian," whispered Albie.

"Do we have any idea where it is?" asked Tim.

"There is this old clue," said Albie pulling a dusty piece of paper out of his bag.

Tim read it:

'Follow flying horses, keep going until they stop,

Once they stop its time to drop,

on to rocks in shallow water'.

"Then, let's follow some winged horses!" said Tim.

"But Tim it's not that simple…" began Albie.

"Amy, Albie wants us to follow flying horses!" called Tim.

Amy didn't reply but did steer towards a herd of winged horses. After half an hour of flying, the horses stopped at shallow water where there were rocks just as the clue had said.

They slid off Storm and explained to Amy what they were going to do. They searched the rocks. After checking for ages Albie sat on a rock and then…

The cliffs parted and a huge waterfall with the purest water appeared before their eyes. It was amazing so they clapped and cheered.

All three of them ran to the waterfall, Amy got a container filled to the brim. Then a deafening roar sounded through the water and a huge dragon that seemed like it was made of water whacked its spiked tail towards Amy but luckily, she ducked just in time.

"It's the Water Dragon! I thought it was a myth." gasped Amy.

"Everything here is a myth!" yelled Tim.

"Amy, what are you doing?!" questioned Albie as Amy ran towards the beast. She did strange movements with her fingers and the brightest flash of blue shot out her hand.

The dragon flew off.

"You just performed the hardest curse ever." babbled Albie.

"Did I? I wasn't sure if I was dreaming," said Amy.

"You were AMAZING!" called Tim.

Amy gave him a small smile and he smiled back.

After filling more containers with the water, Amy whistled for Storm and they all clambered on.

They heard a loud, "AAAAAAAAGGGGH!" and saw Jack falling off a winged horse.

"Jack is alive!" shouted Amy, they swooped over and caught him, and they told him the story. "We best be going Tim," said Albie.

"Ok!" he said as he waved at the others.

"Amy, is there any chance your dragon could singe Tim's hair?" Albie asked. Storm carefully singed it off and Tim had short hair with a streak of red.

They said their goodbyes, got in the taxi and drove until they were back on the streets of New York. They parked outside the mall and Tim's mum was there, she got in. "Nice haircut Tim!" she said.

THE END.

The Magic Poster
by Arthur Moynihan aged 11

The slanting orange door slammed shut on to the faded grey and red 'SECURE SEATBELT' sign. The old, weary man sat down, clutching a small leather bag which was securely fasted with a small patterned rope. The driver glanced dismissively at this, then asked in a bored tone, "So, hard day then, mate?" The man sitting behind him had straggly hair flopping down like a basket of messy clothes, while his tight overcoat was covered in greasy marks, he gave out waves of tedium and jet lag.

The taxi cab itself seemed like it had been lulled to sleep by the dullness of its passenger.
The once merry orange paint had faded and turned brown with decay and inevitable age. Spluttering in protest, the taxis wheels drive slowly out of the airport and squeaked on to the motorway.

He felt sick. He knew he still hadn't answered the driver's question, but he had lost the energy to talk. When he tried to speak, an overwhelming tiredness overcame him, and finally, he fell into the waiting arms of sleep. When he woke up, he was startled to see the taxi had filled up with smoke, and the driver was sitting in the seat next to him!
The driver was staring at him, he then passed his hand gently over the old man's eyes.
He jumped awake after bashing his head as they passed over a bump, and immediately had a burst of relief as he saw that the taxi was not falling apart, and the driver was at the wheel. He must have been dreaming.

Arriving home. He half-heartedly thrust his key into the rusty lock and walked inside feeling sorry for himself. He shook off his wet, grey blazer and threw it in the laundry basket.

The old man had not much to his name, no exciting backstory, no rich family, he was all alone in this world, and as he slumped down on his battered and stained sofa, he felt like, just for a second, he was never going to find hope.

The sad feeling pestered him every day after he came home from his airport job and watched the same movies again and again.

Sometimes he would order a pizza at the weekend and just stay in front of the TV all day.

Today, though, he decided to go out for a walk. His apartment didn't have a garden, so he spent a lot of time indoors, but today, he was going to the London Eye to see his cousin Paul.

He wasn't exactly excited, it was a boring catch up, and when he was on the London Eye, he threw up from eating too many crisps the night before. Once again, he sat down on the same cheap, broken couch, he remembered the taxi and the smoke, and suddenly a thought struck him as he stared up at his peeling ceiling.

What if he could find a way to change his life and gain more money?

He was so excited by this thought that he wrote a list of how to change:

1. Go to bed at 10, no staying up late watching romances.
2. Find healthy food and only ONE McDonalds per week
3. Essential; Find a better job!

He decided to get started on the third one and went cycling all morning around the town looking for work. He was just sitting down and about to give up, but as he slumped down on the beach, above him, there was a blinding flash, a smell of smoke, and a poster appeared on a lamp post that had definitely not been there before. It had fuzzy bright colours, and at first, he thought it was just a silly kid's poster. But he read the big bubbly writing and suddenly he had hope! The advertisement was looking for someone with a bike to cycle around the town delivering post to the elderly. He knew at once that he had to be the one to apply before anyone else did. He saw in small writing that there was an address, the small post office around the corner.

He pushed open the door and heard the familiar ringtone of the bell chiming across the hot room. He had come in unprepared, and when he saw the businessman on his typewriter surrounded by files and cabinets, he suddenly felt beads of sweat trickle down his sleeve one by one. He had never had a professional full-time job before, he was used to coming into the airport and finding there was nothing to clean and being told that he could take the day off. Now he found himself having second and even third thoughts, all coming into his head and staying there, lingering around, eating away at his confidence. What if he wasn't good enough, what if they had found another candidate?

He was just considering going right back out through the silver door when the man noticed him. He seemed unsurprised at the arrival and asked casually, "You here for the job?"

The man stayed silent. "Perfect, just sign here and we are good to go."

The businessman handed him a small paper leaflet with a space for a signature.

The old man was overwhelmed by the response, all the doubts he had been swarmed by seemed ridiculous, and as he cycled back home, he felt happier than he had in ages.

Early the next morning, he got up for his shift and raced around the town on his faithful dark grey bike. Slowly, week by week, his life started to get less and less sad, and he even had a daily routine which included the gym in between lunch and dinner. and a few months into his new healthy lifestyle, he had a call from his old school friend inviting him to spend the summer holiday with him in Egypt.

He got into a small taxi and found the same driver looking back at him,

"OK, mate?" the driver asked.

"Yeah, to the airport please."

As he stepped out of the taxi, he looked back at the familiar face that had welcomed him in and asked.

"How did you do it?" The man just stared back at him, but as he was pulling away, he could have sworn he saw the small makings of a smile.

The Coalfear Cab
by Bella Holland aged 10

Chapter 1: A Narrow Escape

Avery Addington ran for her life from Fynch Wynter. It was clear Avery was going to win.

Avery whistled, and in seconds, 50 wolves surrounded her. Avery was stood on one side of the battleground, Fynch on the other. Wolves were Fynch's one weakness. The only thing that could defeat him.

Except Fynch knew everything that was coming, and immediately cast a bubble around himself. The clock struck midnight, and the wolves disappeared at the sound of their mother's howl.

Fynch struck at Avery using his powers but missed because she dodged out of the way.

Fynch called out for the Coalfear Cab and got whisked away in it.

"Avery, how did it go?" Her mother asked her brightly.

"I lost again. I'll never defeat him." Avery replied.

"Oh, well, didn't you use the Wolves I got you for your birthday?" Her mother asked.

"I did, but their mother called them back."

Then the next morning, there was news floating around the small village called Charitus.

Avery was told that Fynch had gone missing, completely disappeared after he whizzed away in his cab last night. But Avery wanted to just have one match where she could beat him at something. So, there was only one thing she could do. Save him.

Chapter 2: The Journey

Avery set off that night, secretly. She knew where to look from all the rumours she had heard. One person had seen the cab going towards Endover Lake and another saw it heading to the Crystal Lane Bridge. Avery first set off towards Endover. She walked through the Lilac forest. There she found a hollow log and stopped for a break. Avery heard something coming from inside the log, almost howling. Suddenly, 51 wolves dashed out of the end of the log.

"The Truetrap Pack! My wolves!" Avery exclaimed. "Who's messing with my wolves?"

Avery heard a strange noise and jumped. "Hello? Who's there?" Avery said. A boy slightly younger than Avery moved out from behind a tree. "The name's Gillian Partridge. Now, who are you?"

"I'm Avery Addington. And these are my wolves you can't keep them."

"I was supposed to take them to Yuhnhamsadai woods actually. Look, you can have the wolves for 100 follis." Gillian told her.

"I'm not paying a grubby gremlin like you!" Avery said.

"Do you want the wolves or not?"

Avery paid to get her wolves back, she didn't have a choice.

She continued to Endover, towards The Sundune Tower, and finally reached her destination.

Avery searched the lake, but it seemed that if there had been a car it was no longer here.

At sunrise, Avery started getting hungry. But in the blurred distance, she saw a lighthouse on a cliff. She set off.

Chapter 3: The Riverlive Lighthouse

She knocked on the door. "Anyone home?"
"Mother, someone's at the front door!" A voice came from inside. Then a woman in her fifties answered the door.
"Hello, Can I help you? Are you coming to stay at the hotel, or is it something else?"
"A hotel? Perfect! Yes, I'd like to stay here for a night please," Avery said.
"Kathleen! Prepare a room. That's 100 follis for a night. And 20 per meal." The woman said. "Oh yes, my name's Bonnie and I run the hotel with my husband Gordon, and my children Kathleen and Bryan. We run the Riverlive lighthouse."

Avery joined them as they all came to the table to eat dinner together.
"So what journey are you on? Did your mother send you? You're young to be on your own?" Bonnie asked.
"I'm twelve," Avery replied. "And yes, my mother sent me to find my… Father." Avery lied.
"He has a cab, a magic cab, it flies," Avery said.
"Oh, that's peculiar, I saw a cab flying over here at lunchtime! And then I watched it land near the Crystal Lane Bridge!" Bonnie said.

The next morning, Avery was off.
It wasn't too far from the lighthouse. She walked over Crystal Lane Bridge. Then she remembered her real father didn't live too far from there.
Upon Crystal Lane Bridge, stood a man in a fur coat. "Hello," he said in a strong Scottish accent.
"Hello there, I'm looking for A boy of 12 called Fynch, he is a young wizard," Avery said. Suddenly it hit her. This man was her father, she was sure.

"Oh," Said the man. "I was just searching for my son, I was only there for the first few months of his life, and I was wanting him to join my troop."

Chapter 4: The truth

Avery was shocked. Her father, looking for his son?
She had never had any siblings. How could this be true?
"You're Lomhar Addington, aren't you?" Avery said.
"How do you know?" He said, walking down from the bridge.
"Because I'm your lost daughter, Avery Addington."
They glared at each other.
"Father. You're looking for a boy who flew away in a cab, aren't you?" Avery said.
"You really are my daughter, aren't you?" He said.
"I thought my son was looking for me in his magic cab. But you're my long-lost child, and I was looking for you all along, now I've found you, let's find the boy in the cab."

In the middle of a wheat field, was a crashed cab and an injured Fynch.
"Fynch, why did you run away in the first place?" Was the first thing Avery asked Fynch.
"I knew you would eventually win me over with your wolves, so I went to find something better."
Fynch looked down.
"The entire town went berserk! No one knew where you were!" Avery said angrily.
Then her Father spoke. "In fact, do people know where you are, Avery?' I'm taking you both back to Charitus."

"Oh, Avery! My dear! I was really worried!" Her mother exclaimed.

"He just dropped you off? Really! How irresponsible of your father."
"He had to go back home," Avery said.

"I challenge you to a battle, tomorrow," Avery said to Fynch.
"I accept."

Chapter 5: Battle
The battle was on.
Avery threw fireballs at Fynch but missed as he moved out of their way. Avery called her wolves and they quickly arrived, they attacked him and before Avery knew it, he had surrendered.
"And the 1st place prize, the Coalfear cab, goes to Avery Addington!"
Finally, she had her magic flying cab!

Temperature Rising
by Hannah McCormack aged 11

Pulsing red lights, bustling doctors, a metal bed frame.
This is what Toby Andersen saw when he opened his eyes.
Although it hurt to think or exert himself, Toby could formulate one word in his scattered mind: Hospital.
Then his burning forehead pushed its way to the front of his thoughts once more and Toby succumbed to unconsciousness.

Awakening again, perhaps an hour or a week later, Toby saw something, something that was out of place with the orderly hospital environment – a large figure, masked by the shadows. His exceptionally high temperature threatening to sedate him once more, Toby fought to stay awake, out of curiosity. He had good reason to be curious, since there was something bizarre in his ward. And then that bizarre thing stepped into the light, and Toby saw what it was. There, looking almost comically out of place beside the beeping machinery, was a creature. Although it stood on two legs like a person, the resemblance stopped there. Pale, ice blue fur hung from its body like shaggy icicles, with darker blue fur surrounding a small - but strangely kind-looking – face. It had strong, muscular legs that ended in padded paws, and long, bear-like arms. The hands, although similar to a person's, had one finger that was significantly longer than the rest. Its face, with a navy nose shaped similarly to a dog's, had eyes that looked like they were human, and were staring straight into Toby's emerald-green ones.
Now convinced that he was hallucinating (it had happened before, unless there really were turtles at the foot of his bed), Toby stopped fighting his fever, and the tendrils of sleep that pulled at him, and closed his eyes.
That's when he felt it.

The unusually long and cool finger on his forehead, banishing the burning sensation and soothing everything in Toby's body. Feeling refreshed and invigorated, Toby's eyes snapped open. He thought for a moment he saw the lingering stare of those frost-coloured eyes, but then he blinked and saw only the empty ward, and the snow-capped mountains' shadow through the window.

Miracle. Unbelievable. These are the words that surrounded Toby, as medical experts examined him, and nurses stared incredulously at the robust boy who only a week ago had a temperature so high it broke records.

Eventually, Toby got discharged and went back to normal. But he could not shake the feeling that the creature had been real, and he kept thinking he saw it in various places. But he dismissed this as foolish thoughts, until it was impossible to ignore.

Up on the mountain is where Toby saw it for the first definite time since he was in hospital. Their eyes locked for a moment, and an unexplainable feeling passed through Toby – he now knew for certain that it was real. The creature beckoned with that abnormally long finger, and, like a dream, Toby obeyed. He followed the furry shape, up into the peaks of the mountains, noticing that he hardly felt the cold. Eventually, they came to a stop in a small cave nestled between hills of snow, and Toby voiced the question that was on his mind.

"What are you?"

The creature looked at Toby, and in a gruff voice replied, "I am Skarp the Hallbrader." Obviously understanding Toby's puzzled expression, Skarp continued, in a voice that sounded like an ice glacier cracking, to tell his story.

"Hallbraders have been around for centuries. We are healers, for children who need it. Once we heal a child, we stay with them for life and protect them. So, you and I now have an unbreakable bond, and I will help you change the world. I selected you as soon as I saw you in that ward, for I could see that you will make a difference in your adult years." Toby stood, drinking all this information in, he was speechless, his green eyes opened wide in awe.

"What happens now?" he asked, leaning into the blue fur as a gust of wind slapped them with icy fingers.

"We enjoy ourselves!" Skarp quipped, twisting his muzzle in what Toby took for a smile. And they did.

Toby snuck out to meet Skarp in freezing places like the ice rink, or the foot of the mountains. There they played, talked, and built a bond that they believed was unbreakable. But nothing lasts forever.

Toby soon found that he was going higher into the peaks to find Skarp, noticed that his friend seemed uncomfortable in his hot, thick fur, the news always protested about a warming climate, and Toby began to worry. One day he could hold it in no longer, and asked Skarp what was wrong.

"Toby," Skarp started, "surely the climate change situation has not escaped your keen eye, surely you know what's wrong. My fellow Hallbraders have moved further north, but I cannot leave you without your say. The heat is too much for me here." Both pairs of eyes filled with tears. Suddenly, everything Toby had teetered on this decision.

"Go," whispered Toby, breaking the silence. "This is how you will help me change the world."

He kissed the soft blue muzzle, felt the finger on his face, and turned away. When he looked back, Skarp was gone.

Years later, a taxi drew up, a rare sight these days because most cars were banned to stop air pollution. A man with emerald-green eyes stepped out of the cab and began the treacherous climb up the slope. Although he had not been to the mountain in years, his feet remembered the way. From the cave he watched some of the snow melt, wondering about a solution to this problem.

When he came back down, he attended a meeting with other leading scientists. Dr Toby Andersen's plan began to have an impact and it was all driven by his hope that Skarp would be able to live on the mountain once more. Eventually, the world took heed of this message and began changing its destructive ways. In the end, Skarp did help Toby change the world for the better.

Emily and Chloe's Amazing Magical Taxi Adventure Saving Mr Watson!
by Louisa Kennedy aged 9

Emily and Chloe were walking around an old village with Chloe's mum, Sophia Barber.

"Mum? Are we allowed to walk around on our own for a bit?" Chloe asked wanting to be free and have fun with Emily for they don't see each other much anymore, and they wanted to explore this Victorian wonder.

"That would be lovely Mrs Barber!" Emily said making herself clear, she wanted to see the village with Chloe.

"Well, I suppose for 3 hours but remember to stay safe and don't talk to any strangers." Chloe's mum replied, hoping they would stay safe.

"Don't worry Mum we won't be silly!" Chloe laughed. Her laugh was more like a cackle. Skipping down a lane they came across a shop selling antiques quite near the beach.

"This looks interesting." Emily smiled, although it was forced as she didn't really but knew that Chloe liked the look of the shop.

"It does, doesn't it?" Chloe replied happily, as they headed towards the shop. Sadly, for Chloe, it was just closing.

"Oh well! It doesn't matter. After all, it looked a bit run down." Emily said.

"I liked the look of that shop!" Chloe answered glumly.

It was painted hot pink and had many clothes hanging in the window.

"Look over there, a taxi! We can ask for a ride along the seafront. I still have about £50 your mum gave us to spend." Emily cried, trying to cheer Chloe up.

"That would be epic!" Chloe screeched, obviously excited, even though it was just a boring taxi ride.

But things were about to change. They ran up to the taxi, it had no driver but there was a note, 'Help find me and drive the taxi!'

They assumed it meant help the driver (luckily it did). "Shall we get in?" Chloe asked.

"Errm, I suppose, seeing as the driver needs help." Emily struggled to say.

"Who will drive, me or you?" Chloe asked.

"I'll drive. You can't even control a bicycle." Emily responded.

"Rude! But true. Ok, you drive." Chloe cried, laughing at the funny statement.

They climbed into the cab and found that it had a kitchen, a bedroom for two, a bathroom and the driving area doubled as an eating area and living room.

"Wow, this is amazing," Chloe whispered.

"I agree. Totally amazing." Emily actually meant it this time.

"Well, I better get driving!" Emily exclaimed looking at all the buttons.

There was a flying button, a swimming pool button, and loads of buttons to different places. But the best thing was, there was auto drive.

"No point in me driving, I guess." Emily gasped.

The car knew where its owner was and made an announcement. "We are heading to Sydney, Australia, as Mr Watson (this taxi's owner) is there, held by evil scientists doing experiments on him."

"That sounds mad! Surely the sound system must have gone wrong!" Chloe said, her mouth hanging right open. The cab sped up to 10,000 miles per hour, so they got there very quickly.

"Looks like we're here." Emily beamed.

Getting out of the car was not as expected; it kicked you out, like in a weird, superhero movie.

"Are you sure, that we are heading to the right house?" Chloe asked the voice in the car.

"Absolutely!" The car voice chirped.

They walked past famous places, like the Sydney Opera House with those arches. It was lit up at night.

"We can do this!" Emily screamed encouragingly. They passed a place named Experiment House.

"This is it! We have to do this." Chloe walked in first, taking the lead.

"You think you can mess with Mr Watson? If you do, you've got to mess with us first. Charge!" Chloe cried, barging into this creepy looking guy with sticky-uppy hair and a grim face.

"Stop experimenting on these poor people!" Emily snarled.

"Yeah, we're dangerous!" Chloe shouted and did a funny, kick-punch.

"Who on earth are you? And thanks for coming to save me!" Mr Watson jumped in shock.

"We're Emily and Chloe, and we found your taxi and the note asking for help." Chloe smiled and looked at him, then turned into a glare when she looked at the scientist.

"Get out, you silly children!" said the mad scientist with a smirk.

"Then free Mr Watson! You lunatic!" Emily fumed.

"You stupid girl! You think I'm going to let my experiment-person go, just so two little girls will leave?" And the lunatic gave an evil grin.

"Is that so? Game on!" Chloe jumped and headed right towards him. The fight was on. Emily ran and pulled his hair whilst Chloe secretly untied the ropes that Mr Watson was tied with.

"We will be finished with you in a moment, as we already untied Mr Watson!" Emily said, about to give an almighty punch!

Poof!

Together Chloe and Emily kicked and punched him all over so he couldn't move.

"Bye, bye sucker!" Chloe howled. And they left with Mr Watson.

"Thank you, girls, I don't know what I would have done without you." Mr Watson exclaimed. "How did you find my taxi as you don't seem to have Australian accents?"

112

Emily and Chloe told him how Sophia had let them wander around in a town back in England and since the taxi was magic, it drove to the spot where Mr Watson had started from and travelled to Australia.

"Speaking of Mum, we'd better get back to England." Chloe sighed, as they had about 30 minutes left.

"May I come with you as I'd like to get back to my family?" Mr Watson replied.

"Of course! It is your taxi." Chloe gestured, heading towards the car.

"Not anymore. This car moves from owner to owner and if it thinks somebody has been brave and nice then it immediately will become that person's cab." Mr Watson gabbled.

"Does this mean it's ours?" Emily asked excitedly.

"Yes Emily! Anyway, it's both of yours now." Mr Watson smiled eagerly. By this time, they were driving back home, eating loads of sweets from the cab's kitchen.

"We're here!" Chloe screeched. They arrived about 5 minutes early! Quickly they said goodbye to Mr Watson and said hello to Sophia Barber.

"Hi girls. Did you have an eventful day?" Sophia asked.

"Not at all!" Chloe smiled slyly, and whispered to Emily, "Oh yes we did!"

The Cashew Quest
by Alistair Hsiao aged 10

The most extraordinary day of my life… when I - the wonderful Cashew boy - rode in a magic taxi. It was the best feeling ever, almost ineffable.

I actually found the taxi by mistake: I bumped into a hard thing in the dead of night, when I was running from my enemy - the atrocious Almond. He was too fast for me; I couldn't outrun him. By the way, if you didn't already know, Almond is an alien. He is exactly like his name. His body is his armour, it is hard like a shell. His arms and legs are like white roots shooting out. Whenever he wants to go fast, like he is now, he launches himself, putting his legs and arms back into his 'almond' to be more aerodynamic.

Oh no, he just shot a net trap.
Sorry readers, back in a moment…

The atrocious Almond threw the net trap and as quick as lightning, I dodged it. Another millisecond, I would have had no escape. I ran down the road, across the avenue, and up the street. And for my finale, while Almond was preparing for his next attack … I disguised myself as part of the road. When he was out of sight, I made haste and bolted. Then, suddenly, I fell - Almond heard the noise and was hot on my heels.

Panicking, I looked down trying to see the thing I had bumped into - I then had the most terrible shock. There was nothing. I kicked the invisible object with my foot - just to test if anything was there - there was. Then, a head popped out, as if it was floating out of nowhere, it said. "What ya doing kickin' ma taxi mate, if ya wanted a ride ya shoulda just said so, hop in."

I was too shocked to do anything, then I came to my senses and I opened the door of the taxi reluctantly to find lavish leather that was made out of animal skins, dinner trays set fashionably in front of the seat like those in an airplane.

"Come on ya scallywag, git in, whaddya think I am, a waiting person?" said the taxi driver. I needed no second bidding, I clambered aboard in a rush, and we set off. First, I asked the price (it is always best to ask for the price first because once when I didn't ask the price, it cost an arm and a leg).

Surprisingly, the taxi driver only wanted one pound. "That is unexpectedly good value," I said to the driver.

He replied, "Aye it cost nuffin for da refreshments either."

I sat absent-mindedly for a moment and - when I came back to earth - dug in. The steak tasted like pure beef, the milk like pure milk, almost everything had a distinctive taste and was definitely fit for a king: the fruit was zesty, the gammon was meaty, the bread was fresh, you really couldn't ask for anything other than that... After my meal, I sat, content on the sofa-like seat. I began thinking, what is our dear Almond doing right now?

Almond was back on earth, cursing and spitting on the floor. "Another second and I would have got him! Dang and blast, next time I see him, I'll slice him into salami, I'll make him pay!" Then, a sinister plan began to form in his evil mind. "Yes, yes!" he cried, "this will be the way to end him once and for all."

He looked about for another magic taxi, but he couldn't find one, though the magic taxis were everywhere. The reason he couldn't find a magic taxi was because he was evil - only pure-hearted people were allowed to have the honour of going in a magic taxi. So, his plan was wrecked. Poor old Almond.

At that moment, I suddenly realised that we were flying! Yes, really flying! I could see the clouds gathering into a flock below us. I was astounded by the view of the lights illuminating New York City and the malls' lights shining, it was all I could ask for, it looked like a fireworks display, it was wonderful, though I couldn't decide which was more wonderful, the view of New York City or the taxi.

The taxi, I had just realised, had a padded interior which meant that if you crashed, you would be protected. The floor was - hard to believe really - marble, and as slippery as glass, it seemed that the whole taxi itself was made of the finest things in the earth. I celebrated by drinking champagne to applaud the honour of being in this taxi. And don't get me started on the quality of the champagne, its froth was heavenly clouds, and the drink was the finest champagne in the history of champagne.

Finally, we arrived at the destination, but Almond had flown over and spotted me downtown, so I climbed back into the taxi and we set off again.

Almond launched himself like a rocket at me, I dodged, but you should have seen the crater he left. It was as wide as a city and almost big enough to gobble up the entire planet. An idea popped into my head suddenly, I would keep Almond busy by making him go away from land to follow me, then, the city and its people would be safe.

When all seemed lost, I had a brainwave. Without hesitating, I opened the door, snatched out a bottle of champagne, and shook it hard. The froth began to bubble and at once, the bottle began its magic. I aimed the bottle of champagne like a gun, put my finger over the cork to stop it popping when I didn't want it to, took careful aim, predicted Almond's movements, and BANG! The cork flew like a bullet out of a gun and went straight down

Almond's throat. "BULLSEYE!" I cried, dancing a jig while Almond was busy choking.

Police cars came roaring over, sending mountains of dirt blowing across the barren land. "Thank you, Courageous Cashew, this is your best arrest yet, I must congratulate you," bellowed the Superintendent. We went to town and ordered at the best cafe, some macaroons, fresh, luscious, and gooey, along with some Orangeade to wash it down.

"May you be the superhero that defeats all villains!" proclaimed the Superintendent.

And that is the end of my wonderful story.

Josh and the Magic Elves
by Charlie Macfarlane aged 9

One morning, it was just a normal day for a 13-year-old boy called Josh. Josh went to the private school at the other side of the city. It was really far to walk, so he would normally take a taxi, but not on this day. When he went outside, for some odd reason his taxi to school was blue, not the normal yellow. He decided he was just going to walk because, as well as being blue, there was no-one inside, which was really odd. When he was about half-way on his walk to school, the taxi pulled up beside him, and the door swung open.

Josh decided to get inside and see what was going on. When he got in, he checked the front of the taxi, but still, no-one was there. Then he touched something, and the taxi went as fast as lightning and then it suddenly stopped.

Looking around Josh realised that he wasn't in his own city, he was in the mountains

He got out of the taxi and started walking.

When he got to the top of the mountain, he saw a magical city.

Josh was amazed!

There were tons and tons of small scary wee elves with lots of sparkly gold and yummy looking sweets in small sacks.

When the elves saw Josh, they all started charging at him, and then he realised that some of them were military elves because of their suits.

To escape, Josh had to run through lots and lots of obstacles which were all really small. The elves were gaining on him, and then they caught him, and he said, "I come in peace, and I don't know where I am, please help me." The elves said, "ooh, we thought you were here to steal all of our money and sweets!"

"No," said Josh, "I was just going to school and this taxi kept following me and I went inside, and it teleported me here. Then all of you started chasing after me and now we are here." The head elf said, "well, we have been trying to protect all of our money, because every other elf town has been trying to steal it. Last week, an air raid of elves came and destroyed our town, so we had to move here far, far away from any other elf town, but they will find us eventually."

"Well," said Josh, "I can help you if you want, I think I have got an idea!"

Josh took them up the hill to the taxi, and the elves used their magic and transformed the taxi into a huge bus for all the elves to get into. It teleported back to Josh's hometown, and he took them to an old abandoned house. Josh tried fixing the house up a bit, but he had no luck.

Then one of the elves said, "let me try," and the elf used all of his power to fix the house. The house transformed into a beautiful wee cottage for them to all stay in far, far, away from any other elf city.

You never know, the beautiful wee cottage could be the house right next to you! Have you seen any elves lately…?

Video Game travels
by Struan Wallace aged 10

It was a normal day at number 7 Black Avenue, Jamie's dad had gone out to get his new car. Jamie was a very shy boy he had long dark brown hair that went over his bright blue eyes. Jamie did not have many friends and he got bullied at school by some of the older pupils.

He played games on his computer to escape reality. Jamie's mum left him and his dad when he was young for some posh and wealthy man called Percy.

Jamie did not know much about his mum, so he and his dad pretended he did not have a mum.

Jamie's dad is called Ruin, he has short ginger hair and bright blue eyes just like Jamie's. Ruin is an extremely poor man and works as a taxi driver for a company called Wally's Taxis. Jamie's dad was going to get his new taxi from a car dealership called Cars and Parts. Recently there have been lots of missing boys all around Jamie's age.

Jamie was turning 11 next month so he was quite scared because he thought he too might go missing.

When Ruin went out Jamie would always go on his computer.

Ruin thought Jamie was doing his homework, but Jamie was secretly playing his favourite game FIREBALL 2.

FIREBALL 2 is a platform game with different obstacles you need to overcome and mysteries to solve. Jamie loved the game because it felt like a whole new world.

When Ruin got back in his new yellow and navy taxi, with Wally's Taxis painted in bold on the top, Jamie went out to greet his dad. When he got outside his dad walked over to Jamie and hugged him.

"I love it," said Jamie in his quiet voice as he looked at the registration plate it said 'J4M13 RU1N'. Jamie was so happy his heart was exploding. He was pacing left and right and so he went inside to calm down by playing FIREBALL 2. His favourite game.

The next day after getting bullied at school his dad picked him up in his cool taxi which just reminded him how much he liked it. He got in and he hugged his dad and said, "I wish we could afford to go to Madrid, I have seen it in my game."

Suddenly the satnav announced, "destination set, press to travel." Jamie pressed the button before Ruin could stop him. There was a blinding yellow flash and the car teleported to a different location he had never been to before.

Jamie and Ruin looked at each other in confusion, then Jamie realised he was in MADRID!

He said to his dad that he recognised where they were from FIREBALL 2. His favourite game. He asked his dad if he could go outside but Ruin was unable to answer because he was paralyzed with shock. Jamie shouted at Ruin until he came back to his senses.

Eventually, Ruin calmed down and so they left the car for a walk around the streets.

They found an ice cream shop where they bought an ice cream, strawberry of course, as this was Jamie's favourite. They continued to walk around the beautiful sights of Madrid looking at all the attractions. It was starting to get dark, so they started their journey back to the car. On their way to the car Ruin saw an old rusty shed with a sky-blue light coming out of the half open door. They checked it out only to find Ben one of the missing boys from Jamie's school, he was trapped in a light blue force field. Jamie almost didn't recognise him because he looked so different. His clothes were all ragged, his hands and face were dirty, and he looked terrified. He wasn't the happy boy Jamie saw four months ago at school.

Jamie recognised this force field because it was from his favourite game FIREBALL 2.

Jamie knew how to break the force field in FIREBALL 2. He knew you needed to use a dog whistle for 60 seconds. He asked his dad to use the dog whistle app on his phone, they turned the volume up as high as possible and held the phone near the force field. Ruin's phone was old with a cracked screen and Jamie was not sure if it would work. Nothing happened at first but after a few seconds the force field started to vibrate and after a minute passed by it disappeared. Jamie and Ruin grabbed Ben and they ran back to the taxi as fast as they could and got inside.

Jamie said, "I wish we were home."

The satnav said, "destination set, press to travel." Jamie pressed the red button, there was a blinding yellow light, and they were back home. Ben was in shock and did not know what to do.

Jamie, Ruin, and Ben decided to keep their adventure a secret because no one would believe them. Ruin brought Ben back to his home. Ruin knew where he lived because he was a taxi driver. Ben jumped out and ran inside to find his parents. He was so relieved to be home.

Over the next week, Jamie and Ben became good friends and helped each other.

Jamie explained to Ben how playing his favourite game FIREBALL 2 helped him to free Ben. Ben started playing the game too and they would often share tips on how to complete most of the levels.

The Explorers Dream
by Eliot Santell aged 13

I had a strange feeling that the next day would change my life and would threaten to knock down the only sense of security I have ever had. However, this would be a good change. I knew that tomorrow would bring the beginning of a new life, a start of something exciting...

It was just after ten o'clock when I left the dismal building.
I had finally been given a new task as an explorer, from good Ol' Hulda. I had never met her, but she was the head of assignments for 4th year apprentices. I was headed out onto the streets with the map I was given in my left hand.
The directions were written on an aged post-it note, brown at the edges, and not sticky anymore. 'Go to Russia in Moscow'.
That was all, nothing telling me what I had to find. Nothing telling me who I needed to meet. I headed to my favourite restaurant, where I used to work, pondering about what I was going to do, and more importantly, how I was going to do it.
As I stared at the table, I was brought back from my thoughts by the waitress coming over and asking for my order in a snide voice...

For the last few years I had been working at this restaurant, yet still that petty woman was always mean and rude to me for no reason, at least that is what I had told myself, I mean it wasn't like I had taken some of her tips or stolen her promotion, or anything like that. It was not my fault I had gotten promoted instead of her.
Anyways, I was doing well until the manager retired, and his arrogant, demanding son took over. It felt like the end of my life having a 20 something shout at me all day.

But this task to Russia had landed in my lap and it was my way out. I was saved!

I waved down a cab and was about to ask if they could take me to St Pancras Station when the driver tilts her head, looks me up and down, then drives away. What was that about?

I waited until the next one came along, desperately hoping to find a cab as the heavens opened above me. Suddenly, an older-looking black cab pulled up. I knew that often fairies drove these cabs and that I could make a few sales of potions on my way to the station.

Inside, a small pixie-looking driver looked up at me and asked, "need a ride?"

Little did she know, she was where my journey to Russia began. She had soft, mint green hair with vibrant yellow eyes that slightly glowed. She looked about 5 ft 6 and I knew that if the lighting was just right you would see lines on her skin that look strangely like bark.

The girl wore a white turtleneck with ripped jeans. Tattoos covered her hands like gloves.

But what astonished me the most was that she was not like most fairies, she was all alone, normally they stayed in groups, because the more there are, the more powerful they become.

The cab had dark black walls which were slightly iridescent. There was a strange looking indoor windowsill and markings that looked a bit like runes covering the doors and windows.

As I looked at her I suddenly blurted out:

"Hello, my name is Atlas, I was wondering if you could take me to St Pancras?"

She gave me a faint smile and nodded. She had a name tag on her dashboard, but it was dirty, and I could not read her name,

"What's your name?"

She gave me another cheeky smile. I fumbled in my pockets to see what potions and trinkets I could sell in order to cover some expenses on my trip. She glanced in her rear mirror and recognised I was a trader.

"I have some monksbane?" I suggested.

"Perfect, I have been desperately looking for that. I can offer £120?"

The offer was low, but I had nothing else to fall back on. Trading abroad was tough and this was as good as it was going to get.

"Deal!" I exclaimed.

Already, I was thinking of all the things I could buy across the border. With no proper instructions, an empty bank, and an excited mind, this was the adventure every explorer would dream of.

Making a living by selling your stash of goods and trading with fairies… My love for travelling was an itch that always had to be scratched. I had always had an urge to go East, but my 9-5 jobs kept me trapped like a mouse stuck in a cage.

But this time, I took the leap. This time, I did it. There was no turning back and no stopping…

Suddenly, I jolted from an unexpected sleep. The excitement and amazement of this new chapter in my life must have brought a blanket of exhaustion over me.

Looking out of the cab window, it took a few seconds for my sleep-ridden eyes to realise that I was no longer in London. There was not a single dark cement building anywhere in my foggy sight. There was no bleak, boring, train station.

However, I was still in the small, plump, old, black cab. The beautiful buildings around me displayed an array of different patterns and colours, it was nothing like I had ever seen before. I could not wait to look around, explore this weird place's markets, I jumped out of the taxi, when suddenly I remembered Hulda.

"Wait," I turned to look at the fairie.

"Welcome to Moscow, Atlas." Said the driver.

It was Hulda. She was my task giver, my boss. How did I not realise, it was so obvious?

"Why am I here Hulda?"

"Because you are returning home."

I had no clue what she was talking about, so I asked again.

"Why am I here?"

"Don't you know why you always had the desire to travel East?" She inquired.

Obviously, I didn't, and she knew I kept coming back for more tasks, always asking about tasks in the East.

"I didn't think you noticed my desires."

She frowned as she heard the sarcasm in my voice.

Suddenly, she started smirking. She leaned through the window, she brought her face so close to mine that I could feel her breath against my cheek, then she whispered four words almost too quiet to hear…

"Welcome home…your majesty."

Then she drove away…

The Flying Taxi
by Selina Scally aged 9

It was a hot Sunday morning in August. Grandad's taxi sat alone and tired in the driveway after a busy week. Freya, my little sister, and I were sitting on the front doorstep with nothing to do. Freya looked over towards the taxi. "Maybe we could play in Grandad's taxi, he won't notice," she said. "OK, " I said. We walked over and pulled on the door. It was open, so we got inside. Freya clambered onto the driver seat, and I sat shotgun. We were pretending we were in a colossal, lightning bolt race, overtaking and crashing into cars. Just then, my attention focused on a big, bright red button, that was hidden very well, at the side of the driver's seat. I called over to Freya who was turning the steering wheel frantically and crashing into 'more cars.'

"Freya! Look! There is a bright red button at the side of your chair! What do you think it does?" I asked. "I am going to push it!" said Freya. "No, we might get in trouble," I shouted. But it was too late...

The car moved slightly, then lifted from the ground. "Wow!" we both said with surprise.

"Freya, why did you push that button, now we are floating in the air!" I screamed.

Freya turned the steering wheel. All of a sudden, the whole car turned. "Cool," said Freya, excitedly. The car had continued to rise, and we were above the houses. Freya straightened up the steering wheel and put her foot on the accelerator! We jerked forward, then started to move speedily over the clouds. "Freya, take your foot off the pedal now!" I shouted. Freya did as I told her and the taxi slowed. We began drifting towards the ground.

I looked out of the window. I could see large trees and thick green plants. I leaned over and pressed the red button, but this time nothing happened. I pressed it again, still nothing. I pressed it a third time, a little more angrily, it didn't work. The taxi reached the ground.

Freya and I opened the doors and climbed out. "What will we do now?" Freya exclaimed.

I noticed a long, smooth, stone path that lead further into the woods. "The path is our only chance to get back home. We might find someone who can help us," I said to Freya. Freya nodded. We held hands and made our way down the path.

Meanwhile, back at Granny and Grandad's house, Grandad was scratching his head, wondering where on earth his taxi had gone. Granny began screaming and searching frantically around the house for us. Granny said, "Stop worrying about your stupid taxi and start worrying about where Selina and Freya have gone!"

"I thought they were in the house with you," said Grandad.

Grandad suddenly held his chest as he realised what might have happened. He knew what his taxi's red button could do! He sneaked away quietly while Granny was still frantically searching for us.

Grandad climbed into his old, rusty, Austen 10 that had been sitting in the garage. It made a bang and a roar as he started the engine. He drove it out of the garage. It chugged and filled with smoke as it moved. "Come on old man," said Grandad as he pushed a similar red button under the seat. The car began to levitate, and off Grandad went in search of us.

Freya and I had found our way to an old red barn with a leaky, brown, wooden roof. We pushed open the large gate and crept inside. "Horses!" said Freya. I turned around and there were two horses, one light brown and one dark brown, crunching on hay. I began petting the dark brown horse when, all of a sudden, a voice came from the horse, "Yes that's the spot."

Freya and I got such a fright that we fell backwards.

Then the horse said, "Sorry I should have introduced myself, I'm Toffee and this is Fudge."

"Does Fudge talk too?" asked Freya.

"Of course, I can talk," came a voice from a small distance.

128

"We want to go home, but we don't know where we are. Can you help?" I asked.

"You're in Dulkins farm," Toffee said.

"Are we still in Scotland?" I asked.

"Yes," said Toffee and I felt relieved.

"Can you take us home?" I asked.

"Yes, come on." We climbed up onto the horses' backs. We left the barn and started to ride around the field.

While we were with the horses, Grandad had found the taxi and he was looking around for clues to where we had gone. He left the old car and began driving the taxi down the stone path. Grandad was worried, he had heard stories of children that had been lost in this area. Some say a witch had turned them into horses. As Grandad turned the corner, he saw us riding the horses. He shouted, "Get off those horses!" from the car window.

Freya and I heard Grandads voice. "Stop!" we shouted to the horses, but they ignored us and kept galloping.

"We have to get to Gretta, so she can turn these girls into horses, and then she might set us free," said Fudge to Toffee.

Freya and I were terrified. "Grandad help!" we screamed.

I saw a figure of a green, misty woman at the door of an old, creepy, stone cottage. We were getting closer. Grandad was hovering above us in his taxi wondering what to do. Just then the taxi lost control, crashing down on top of the witch's house, and killing her. As the witch died, the horses turned into little boys and we all tumbled to the ground.

Grandad got everyone into his taxi, which was bizarrely unharmed by the crash, and towed his old car with a rope attached to the back. As he pressed the red button, he told the boys, "I know where you live. Your disappearance is all over the papers. Your mum is worried sick about you both."

He flew them straight home. We saw from the car how ecstatic their mum was to have them back.

As we flew home in the taxi, Grandad said, "Do me a favour Selina and Freya, don't tell anyone about the red button, and don't be pressing it again." Freya and I looked at each other and smiled.

The Three Miracles
by Rachel Harwood aged 11

It was a cold, dingy night. Clouds gathered, snow threatening to burst from the skies. People hurried along icy paths, heads down, wrapped in hats and scarves. Inside the cosy cottages that lined the cobbled streets, bright fires danced in ashy grates, stockings hung over joyful flames.

Outside, a man, wearing a tweed suit and navy tie, slipped and skidded along the path. He put his hand into the pocket of his trousers - his numb fingers fumbling. A soft jingle let him know he had found his keys. He rounded a sharp corner and slotted them into the lock. The lock clicked. He opened the door and stepped inside the welcoming, warm cottage. Bang. The door slammed shut from a sharp, gusty breeze. A jittery woman, ran to meet him, all in a fluster. It was Christmas Eve, and she was going to stay with her family, but the taxicab was nowhere to be seen.

Many miles away, a man sat, tapping his freezing fingers on the cold steering wheel of his old black taxi. Ahead, a crew of people were moving a drift of dirty snow off the road. The driver inspected his gold pocket watch that he had been given many years ago. It was 9:03 pm. He was 15 minutes late. He tapped his feet to try and keep the blood circling and prayed that they would finish quickly.

All of a sudden, a bright flash of blue light streaked across the dark sky. A pale mist descended over the road. The man jolted upright, heart thumping. He strained his eyes trying to make out the mysterious figure inside the light. He could see an old woman, dressed in a blue floaty dress, stood in the centre - her hair in an elegant blonde bun. The driver blinked hard. He was sure he recognised her, but from where? The lady was daintily holding a stick with swirls and patterns carved carefully into it. The memories in his brain suddenly fell into place. She looked suspiciously like the fairy godmother from his childhood fairy tale book. No surely not – it was only a story.

As quickly as she came, she disappeared, leaving a clear road ahead. Stunned, the driver sat, staring into space, trying to work it all out. A loud honking erupted from the car behind him. Hurriedly he snapped out of his thoughts and drove off. High above the godmother smiled. With a flick of her wand and a swish of her skirt, she evaporated into the night.

A couple of minutes later, the taxi pulled in front of the fretful lady's house. Almost immediately, the lady ran out, only pausing to give her husband's weary cheek a quick peck. The taxi driver, whose name was Robert, tensed, seeing the woman's furious face. As soon as the door was open, the lady started ranting. On and on about being late. Robert was in for a very long night.

Eventually, the angry lady fell asleep with exhaustion and Robert breathed a great sigh of relief. All of a sudden, the snow that had been threatening to pounce for hours fell from the dark sky. It swirled and danced in front of the cab, covering the windows until Robert could only see a blanket of white. He looked at his clock, 10:03 pm. A bright light flashed through the air, silvery-white. Robert jumped, startled his heart pounding like a wild horse. In a second, the snow cleared from his taxi. The whooshing stopped silence reigned. A tall figure with hair as black as ebony, skin as white as snow, and lips as red as blood stood in the centre of the road. She winked then disappeared. "What?" murmured Robert disbelievingly. Before he could think, the snoring woman woke with a start.

"Why on earth have you stopped your silly taxi in the middle of the road? Drive!" she yelled, her face red and furious. Robert muttered a quick apology and drove on through the mysterious world.

As he drove, the woman huffed irritably – furious that she was late. After a while, they came to a bridge. The wall was low, and the road busy – and very icy. Most people were also going to see their family which meant there were many vehicles using the bridge. Without realising what was happening, Robert's wheel connected with another vehicle, and they both careered around until a dreadful thing happened. A strong gust of wind tipped the taxi over the side.

They fell. Plummeting down, down, down, the ice coming closer and closer. Robert had no control – he knew this would finish them off. The lady beside him burst into frantic tears wailing forlornly – all her annoyance forgotten. This would be the end of her life. Why hadn't she said goodbye properly to her beloved husband, who patiently put up with her frequent whining? She blamed herself for this accident, if she hadn't been so hateful to this taxi driver – she was sure none of this would have happened.

Roberts heart leapt into his throat, his gut twisting. As they neared the ice, he let out a piercing scream, the woman joining in. Together, they screamed until their throats were dry. Just as the nose of the cab connected with the cracking ice, the digital clock on the dashboard flipped to its's final second and froze, stating 11:03 pm, out of the broken shards of ice, something rose up - three furry bears with water dripping off their backs. The first one was biggest, holding the others aloft on his shoulders. The medium bear held - high above her head – a little bear. On top was a young girl with fair, long hair- Goldilocks. With one massive push, they all heaved the petrified troupe back up to the bridge.

Half an hour later, the lady was warmly greeted by her mother and treated to a cup of tea and Robert jumped into bed beside a comforting hot water bottle and tried not to wonder what on earth had happened.

Evie
by Emily Locke aged 10

Evie climbed out of the taxi and trudged along in the snow into an empty alleyway. She wore her usual baggy jeans, purple coat, turquoise beanie, and matching turquoise gloves. She had short blonde hair that shimmered like the sun and she had eyes as blue as the ocean. She was twelve years old. She looked around and spotted some wanted posters up on the wall. On them had an old man with white hair and a white beard that was ridiculously small, he was smoking a cigar and had on a black suit.

Just then she heard a click from behind her and she swung around, fast as a cheetah. There was a doll in the shop window. Identical to the one she used to have at home, the one she had to put in the bin, the one that had a pretty blue petticoat with a big hat and bow tied around it…she looked around her, half expecting one of her friends to jump out. She waited for a few minutes, but no one came.

She ran up to the shop window and the doll was gone. Completely vanished. She skimmed her eyes over the shop through the window. Suddenly she caught sight of the doll. On the table beside the incredibly old till, in the left corner. Feeling panicked she ran over to the door and tried to pull it open, but it wouldn't budge. She was livid but full of curiosity. Why was there a doll identical to the one she threw out? Why had it moved like that? The thought of this made her panic again and she gave up and slowly walked away. Just then she heard a creak, she turned and saw that the door had opened! There was a man standing at the door and the funny thing was he looked exactly like the man in the wanted posters.

He smiled and said, "Come in I have been expecting you." But it wasn't a happy smile it was more of a sly one. She slowly walked in. She was taken into a small room and the man said, "take a seat, I am Mr Evans."

She sat down on a MASSIVE velvet armchair that had a beautiful golden rim around the edge. She looked around the spacious room it had pictures from the world wars and some of Victorian ladies and men, it had purple wallpaper, a massive orange carpet, and a big wooden chest of drawers. The strange man walked out of the door and came back half a minute later, carrying a small wooden chest. As he sat down on the chair in front of her, he opened the chest slowly, and in it was a thin string with gems on one end of them he pulled one out and passed it to Evie.

He said, "take care of this and bring it back tomorrow." Evie found that her head was nodding before she could say anything.

"Before you leave. If you cannot find me or this shop tomorrow just wait in front of where you last saw it."

Evie ran all the way back to her friend's house (her family was staying there because her house was getting an extension).

When she got back everyone was in the middle of eating dinner. She looked outside and suddenly it was dark. She hadn't noticed that before.

She went back outside, and it was light. But not for one second did she think that the mysterious crystal had anything to do with it. She ran back inside to her bedroom. Her bedroom was white with a black carpet and was VERY cluttered. She flopped on her bed and took out her phone but couldn't concentrate because she was so jumpy. Who was this man? Was she going to go back to the shop tomorrow? She took out the crystal that he had given her and examined it. It was pure white and when she examined it closer, she saw it had her name engraved in it! What did this mean? She spent the rest of the night playing on her phone. Just then she heard a knock at the door and her friend came in. "Hi Evie, are you okay? You have been hiding in here for AGES," said Sophia.

"Oh, be quiet you are starting to sound just like my mum," said Evie in a slightly grumpy way.

Sophia giggled, "I guess you're okay then." and she disappeared back out the door.

The next day Evie made her way out in a taxi, it took a frightfully long time just to arrive at her destination. She made her way along the alleyway and stopped where the shop should be, but it wasn't. She waited for a couple more minutes. Suddenly there was a HUGE blast of wind and snow, Evie covered her eyes for protection. When the snow cleared there stood the shop just like it had always been there! Mr Evans came out the door acting like nothing had happened. He took her inside and she followed him into the small room again.

He said, "I travel through time so I can catch people like you, to give ME more time to live." Evie was starting to get concerned.

"The stone I gave you will be your home for the next century before it runs out of power," he said in a VERY sly voice.

Suddenly he stood up and started forming into a horrible looking monster. He had a grey slimy face, horrible fangs, slimy feet, and distressing sharp points coming out of his arms. He lunged at her and she dodged out the way, while still holding onto the stone but just then the stone rolled out of her hand and Mr Evans caught it! He held it up to the light and everything began to swirl around him, including Evie.

Suddenly it all stopped, and Evie could see she had been sucked inside the jewel, with no way out.

All that dreadful day she had a search party looking for her but of course, they wouldn't find her. Not until the next century...

Josh and the Magic Taxi
by Daniel Gawish aged 10

One snowy, cold, wet Saturday an old man called Josh was listening to the news about the weather in his dark apartment.

Large amounts of snow were forecast.

It had already begun to fall and was whispering through the screeching wind. In his apartment there was a small, hard, oak bed, a big pile of toilet roll, and a big brown piece of paper, he had not noticed the paper before. He picked the paper out from under the oak bed and looked at it. It was a treasure map and at the bottom, it said, 'from the original owner Ya Hairy'.

Josh immediately set off in his rusty old car to go and look for the treasure.

It appeared to be in Wellington, the capital of New Zealand.

He did not get far, his car broke down because it could not cope in the snow, so he called a taxi and after five minutes the black taxi with five seats arrived. He got in and asked, "may I go to Manchester airport please?"

This is where the map told him to start.

The driver said, "yes," and they began talking.

Josh mentioned a recent holiday in Canada and before he knew it, the taxi had teleported them to the capital of Canada, Ottawa. Josh quickly discovered that this was not just any taxi, but it had magical powers, and it was a teleporting device. He realised that by saying the name of a country he could teleport there.

Josh decided to have some fun with this but Phil the taxi driver did not want to join him

Phil pushed a button and teleported back to his home giving Josh full control of the magic taxi.

Josh knew he wanted to go to Wellington but decided to see some places along the way. He travelled to Greenland where he came across polar bears swimming happily, India where he saw elephants stomping around and calling to each other loudly, and Ireland where he saw leprechauns dancing!

After Ireland he asked the taxi to go to Scotland to visit the highland cows, but it does not work! After too many uses of the car, it must have eventually worn out. Josh is now in Ireland 11,596 miles away from Wellington where the treasure is supposed to be.

Josh sat thinking about what to do next when a leprechaun came over to talk to him. Josh could not believe his eyes or ears - he found himself talking to a small, red headed, plump leprechaun wearing a green jacket and a four-leaf clover in his black hat.
The leprechaun, called Patrick, asked Josh if he needed any help. Josh explained that he has found a treasure map and would like to go and get the treasure in Wellington, but he has no way to get there.
Patrick asked him if he needed one of his winged unicorns to fly there. Patrick calls over a unicorn, it has rainbow hair with a fifteen-inch glowing horn. "Y-y-yes please," Josh stuttered.

They immediately take off into the big cloudy sky and WOOOOOOOSH they went as fast as a jet and eventually they arrived in Wellington. Josh found the next clue in a dark cold, wet alleyway.
It said, 'you are close, but you are too low, look high'.
That could only mean one thing - it must be on top of a skyscraper. Could it be on top of The Majestic Centre, the tallest skyscraper in Wellington? Excitedly, Josh climbed slowly to the top to investigate. After hours of climbing, he finally found the treasure and opened it. It was fifty-three diamonds and five billion-pound notes (£££!!!) and three mobile phones.

He was so overwhelmed and excited he sold his old dark apartment and buys a mansion with a swimming pool, table tennis table, a massive bed, and a cinema room. He also brought a Lamborghini and a Ferrari. Now he loves everything he bought and is such a happy, rich nice man.

The Craziest Day Ever!
by Emily aged 10

Hi, my name is Hayley, this is my diary, and today my new friend is coming round. I met her on holiday in Hawaii, I had so much fun in Hawaii! But I did spend most of my time in the pool there, instead of with all the other kids in the kids' club.

My friend is called Ella. She is quite tanned, and she has brown hair, but we can talk about her later let's introduce me for now.

As you probably know, my name is Hayley but what you won't know is that I'm eight years old and have pale skin and my hair is blonde. Today, I am wearing a pink top with a silver sparkly love heart I am also wearing denim trousers with rips in them. My hair is at the perfect length for me, it is under my ribs.

I was so excited when the doorbell rang, it was Ella, we were going to bake fairy cakes and everything!! When I opened the door, I saw Ella in a really nice pink skirt. Tucked into it was a white top with black dots, her hair was braided and was down to under her ribs, just like me! Behind her was a taxi cab. The taxi cab looked different in some way; it was blue, normally taxi cabs are yellow or black but blue was something else. Anyway, let's just talk about the playdate.

First, we went up to my room to play with my toys and decide what to do. In the end, we decided to play truth or dare. I did truth on Ella and I found out her favourite food is pretzels. When she said the word, "pretzels," my mouth watered really badly.

After truth or dare, we made fairy cakes. There was a magical mystery item that we used that was not part of the recipe. We thought that it would do no harm but when we put it in, the mixture started to bubble. I was scared for a minute but then it stopped bubbling which was weird. When the fairy cakes were ready, my mum took them out of the oven. But for some reason, she looked surprised, so I went over to see what was wrong and the fairy cakes were PINK!!!!!! PINK!!!!!! I think that was the secret ingredient that did that. When my mum left, me and Ella took a bite out of a fairy cake and you will never guess what we turned into...

Ok, here is the big reveal. We turned into, wait for it...FAIRES!

Yes, you heard me FAIRES!

I was a little scared but at the same time really excited.

Of course, I didn't tell my mum because if I did it would just ruin the whole excitement.

Also, I would get in trouble and Ella would need to go home. When my mum came back, we hid in the garden. When we went outside, we discovered we could fly, it was great fun, but I got carried away and crashed into my treehouse and broke my wings!!

It was embarrassing especially in front of my new friend Ella. I was also really upset when my wings broke because Ella laughed at me and to make things worse, she flew into the house and stole my diary.

Hi, my name is Ella. Hopefully, Hayley has already introduced me, if you don't remember me, I'm the girl with the odd-looking blue taxi. Don't judge me please just because my parents are kind of one the richest people in the world. Well, not as rich as the King and the Queen but you know what I mean. I was on holiday in Hawaii, you probably already know that because Hayley will already have told you that in her secret diary that I am writing in right now, which is actually really fun. Oh no, Hayley is coming, I repeat Hayley is coming! Hah, my mistake, it's not her. This is really fun, Ella is going to be really angry that I've read and written in her secret diary, but I don't really care! I've had a fun day here with Ella, but her house is so small compared to mine, they obviously don't have as much money as my rich family. I have a much nicer bedroom and Hayley's stuff is so cheap and babyish. Oh, that sounds like Hayley coming now and she sounds angry. Maybe I should have stayed and helped her down from the treehouse. Who am I kidding of course I shouldn't have. Hey, I think I am no longer a fairy. Boring!

I AM SO ANNOYED RIGHT NOW FOR LOTS OF REASONS AND THAT IS WHY MY WRITING IS SO BIG AND IT WILL PROBABLY STAY LIKE THAT UNTIL I CALM DOWN. FIRST OF ALL, THIS IS ME, HAYLEY, IN CASE YOU DIDN'T KNOW BECAUSE ELLA HAS BEEN WRITING IN MY SECRET DIARY AND SHE SAID SOME MEAN THINGS ABOUT MY HOUSE AND TOYS. I NEED TO CALM DOWN, I AM SO CROSS WITH HER!

Ok, I think I'm ok now, so the other thing that made me REALLY annoyed was that when I found her with my diary, she threw it across the room and smashed my favourite picture.

When I got upset, she just laughed and said it was a horrible picture anyway, which was not a nice thing to say. At this point, I got my dad's phone and called Ella's mum and asked her to send her, "special blue cab" to come back and collect Ella to take her home.

Ella had been nasty and rude. I think that the lesson for today is that Ella is not the kind of person I thought she was, and I don't think we should be friends anymore.

In the City
by Samuel Au aged 10

It was another busy day in Manhattan.

There were lines of traffic everywhere you looked, and the bustling wind filled the air with a chill like a cold, spine-tingling secret.

Driving through Times Square was never an easy task. You had to keep your eyes alert for potential customers and other drivers with no mercy. Not to mention the continuous whining of passengers in the back.

"This is my stop!"

"Could you please answer me?"

"Is there anybody in there?"

What I needed was an adventure, something that would take me to a foggy castle wearing shiny armour with knee-high boots that sparkled, complete with a damsel in distress.

The customer in the back was scrolling through her phone, the great landmarks and buildings missed for some silly picture of a grumpy cat. She had long, coal-black hair and thick glasses that rested on her cheeks. Her fuchsia pink socks covered her knees and she looked like she had just been to a fancy-dress party.

Much to my dislike, we were about to go round a corner. I hated corners. You never knew what was going to jump out at you - cars, lorries, and sometimes even dogs!

Thankfully, it was now late Sunday afternoon, and the sidewalks of New York were deserted. No one was going to use the zebra crossing, it's paint old and worn out.

There was a flash of light. I rubbed my eyes. A busy day's work had knocked the life out of me. I looked intensely at the road ahead. There was something or someone on the crosswalk. Whatever it was, was too small to be human.

It was camouflaged almost perfectly against the gravelly road. Two small specks of yellow that looked like beads of lemon drops circled the crossing. I brought the cab to a sliding, screeching halt narrowly avoiding the ghostly figures.

Cautiously, I dangled my feet out of the car onto the road. Like a jaguar stalking its prey, I tip-toed towards the black figures. Four beady sapphires twinkled as they looked up at me. I chuckled at the situation. What I was so afraid of turned out to be………. two baby penguins!

I scooped them up. After ten years of being a taxi driver, I knew where they came from, the amazing Central Park Zoo. It would be rude of me not to give them a ride home. The inquisitive pair jumped out of my arms into the taxi. The girl in the back spat out her coffee painting the interior different shades of brown. Happily, the penguins sat in the two available seats and after a lot of calming down, the girl in the back strapped them in. The penguins both responded by giving her a love nip which made her look like the happiest person in the world.

Looking in the mirror, I realised that the penguins had small name tags attached to them with a thin piece of string.

"There's something around their legs, what does it say?" I asked.

"Potato and umm Ping!" she replied enthusiastically.

The thought of penguins having names was ludicrous to me but after a while, it made more sense. Who doesn't have a name?

"Nearly home!" I exclaimed to Ping and Potato.

"Squawk!" they replied.

"Back to mummy!" the girl reassured them.

In a rush to get to the zoo, we were going way over the speed limit. People were honking loudly at us and the penguins would just squawk at them with pure annoyance on their faces. The girl didn't seem to mind that I wasn't taking her to her destination. She was too busy taking pictures of Ping and Potato.

144

The sky darkened as it was drawing nearer to sunset. We were only a mile away from getting Ping and Potato home but still faced a race against the clock. The gates would be closing any minute.

Hearing loud roars and growls coming nearer and nearer, we had finally made it to the zoo.

The penguins wobbled out of the car like a jelly, past the red pandas, past the grizzly bears, and past the… "Squawk!"

A loud, fluffy bird with a bright yellow crest raised its head and stared wide-eyed at Ping and Potato. She let out a second screeching squawk that sounded like a car engine starting up and marched towards them. The penguin chicks jumped onto the railings and squeezed through a tiny hole in the fence. Reunited, they all opened their wings and hugged each other tightly. The once icy breeze slowly turned warm and gently touched our faces while we observed the three heads lovingly rubbing against one other. Nothing was as magical as this mother's love for her children.

The Adventures of Intrepid Isidora
by Isidora Holms aged 10

Hi, my name is Isidora. You don't hear that name much do you?

My mum is a professional designer and today my dad is in America for work. I love America. My mums' side of the family lives there.

Today is exciting. I get to be the model because my mum is designing kid's clothes but the only bad thing about it is that I needed to wear a white vest and white leggings.

So, I had to get out of what I was wearing. I was wearing blue turquoise leggings and pink shoes. It was my favourite outfit, but anyway I changed into my boring white top and leggings.

As usual, I went downstairs and had fruit loops for breakfast.

"Yum, yum."

Then I went over to Coco (my fluffy cute dog) and stroked her.

Mum shouted to me from upstairs, "we're going now."

"Okay," I shouted back.

I ran to get my phone and got my favourite jacket on. It was nice and fluffy (like Coco) on the inside of it. I ran to say bye to Coco. I heard the door open, so I ran to catch up with my mum.

We walked downstairs and looked outside; it was pouring with rain. It looked wild as if there was a storm on the ocean.

So, we ran back and got 2 umbrellas, opened the door and ran over to the taxi cab, and asked the lady to take us to the Model Act office. She didn't know where it was, so we gave her the directions and we set off. On the way, we saw a magician performing on the pavement.

The lady told us that we were there in a squeaky voice.

We got out of the taxi and ran into the office. I was filled with excitement and ran upstairs to get started…well to be honest what did I get started on? Standing still!

Okay…. Sorry, bad joke but back to the story. I thought it would be fun, but it is the most boring thing in the world doing nothing.

However, I like watching my mum make clothes.

My dream job is to open a horse stable, very random, isn't it? It took a while but in the end, it was fun seeing the results of her work. The clothes were amazingly beautiful.

I was hungry, so we went out for lunch and went to get Taco's, they were so good.

After lunch, my mum had to go to a clothes shop without me so sent me home in a taxi. When I got in the taxi cab, there was a weird lady driving and she was all covered up. Five minutes passed in the taxi and her hat was slowly falling off. I saw that her ears were as long as a fairy's ear. Then my mind went blank. When my eyes opened, I was in a fairyland full of unicorns, elves, pixies, fairies, goblins, and dwarfs.

There were sweets growing from the tree-like candy apples, candy cane, corn candy, rock candy, and gumballs. It was amazing so I went to explore and started running. There was a sign, with a picture, that said, 'Wanted'.

I looked to see who it was…IT WAS ME! Why would people be looking for me? So, I started to look for a place to hide and I climbed up a tree. I was a bit hungry, so I picked a gumball off the tree and ate it. I sat up there for a while then I decided to move tree as the next tree had rock candy. I had to try some of it. It was better than the ones they sold at the shop back home. Suddenly, I heard some elves coming so I tried to be as quiet as a mouse but then the branch broke and they saw me and started coming to get me. I couldn't run in a tree, could I? Then I thought I was in a fairyland so maybe I could fly so I whispered to myself, "I can fly, I can fly," and it happened. I was flying.

How do you fly? It is hard work but it kind of worked okay, anyway the Elves couldn't get me now I hoped. I had to get away further.

I saw a nice sandy beach so I flew over there and thought maybe I could turn into a mermaid.

I jumped in but sadly I didn't turn into a mermaid.

I was splashing around in the water when I felt something weird on the sandy floor, so I scavenged along the sand and found a ring. It was pale blue, and it shimmered in the sun like a beetle's shell. I decided to put it on. When I put the ring on it sparked and instantly, I was a mermaid.

How cool! So, I went to play with the dolphins and fish and looked around for an hour or two. Then I came back up to the surface and took the ring off. The sparkle happened again, and I was human. I went back to the taxi and the weird lady with the elf ears said that we were home.

I paid her then ran into the house and went to get some tea.

I think I know why the elves wanted me. I must have been an intruder to their land, and they didn't know who I was. But who doesn't know me? ... Intrepid Isidora.

The Berry, The Breath and The Bark
by Dylan Wade, aged 11

It was a regular Tuesday afternoon, Ralph and Johnny were returning from school (Thinmbleton Primary School – which is the worst primary school in the UK) in their taxi when all of a sudden, it sped as fast as it could down a dark, damp and gloomy alleyway into a wall.

What was going to happen? Would they survive? Without warning, the car drove faster and faster, each second feeling longer and longer, until the wall was no more. In an instant, they had entered a mysterious land... There were GIANT mushrooms!

Some people were walking around, they were tiny, holding pickaxes and had beards and... they were in Fairy-tale Village!

The mushrooms were homes, and the small beaded people were dwarves! The boys knew that the only way to get home was to find someone who looked very wise; so that was what they did.

After searching for hours, they found a man (who was very wise) who told them that the only way to get home was to create the Potion of Perfection. They needed Nokiong berries from the deepest of swamps, defended by Orlong, the ogre of oblivion, and the breath of Melissa, the dragon of Fairy-tale Village, the most feared thing across the village, who spent her time guarding the malevolent maple, a tree that comes to life if anyone stands in its path. Of which they needed some of its bark.

Ralph and Johnny were told to come back to the wise wizard to create the Potion of Perfection. They would have to pour it over the taxi's steering wheel to drive through the wall, so they could get back home and live their regular lives again.

Off they set, on their new adventure to get back home.

It was a treacherous journey to the swamp. With every step that they took, it felt like they were one step closer to victory and one step closer to getting home and eating baked beans and sausages.

Just before they reached the swamp, a bee (who was called Barry) buzzed over and explained to Ralph and Johnny that he was once a human too, but he had been trapped in Fairy-tale Village for too long. So, he had been transformed into a mythical creature – a talking bee. He said to the boys that if they didn't escape in time, then they would become mythical creatures as well. The boys were worried as although they didn't know what they would be, they knew that it wouldn't be human.

Barry wanted to see the world again, so he offered to help Ralph and Johnny on their quest to reach home. Together they reached the deepest of swamps and they saw it, the much needed Nokiong berry. It was pink and plump, but it had blue speckles all over.

Although they were brightly coloured, they grow very low down, so they were almost impossible to see in the mud of the swamp.

Luckily, Barry, being a bee, was able to spot the berries submerged within the depths of the swamp.

But they had forgotten all about Orlong the ogre (who terrorised anyone he saw) and as the creature rose up Ralph, Johnny and Barry were in the clutches of fear.

Would they be able to survive? Johnny was the first to find his senses. He kicked the Ogre hard and shouted. "Run!"

Quickly, they found a cave to hide in from Orlong, little did they know it was Orlong's cave!

Without warning, the beast entered his home, shouting in pain with each step that he took.

Luckily, Orlong was too busy nursing his sore leg to see them, so they all ran again, and they left the cave alive.

Ralph had kept the Nokiong berries in his hand. The first part of their quest had been completed.

Unfortunately, that was the easiest challenge that they would face.

With the berries safely tucked away in Ralph's backpack, the boys and the bee found shelter under a tree, hidden from any dangers that could come their way. Before they knew it, the night was over; they had rested their heads and were ready to accomplish the next part of their mission. Next, they needed to find the dreaded dungeon of Melissa, the dragon of Fairy-tale Village. Climbing over mountains, crossing over plateaus, supplies were low, but they still had good spirits and a positive mindset.

After a long hike (and many complaints) their eyes lay upon the dungeon of Melissa. Before entering the lair, they saw some barracks were close by. They headed there and took bottles to capture dragon's breath, armour to protect themselves, swords in case they needed to slay the dragon, and an axe to take off the bark of the malevolent maple tree.

Courageously, they entered the dungeon with their hopes high.

They knew turning back was not an option, it was either them or the dragon. Nobody could stop them now, they had to go in.

There she was, Melissa, (the dragon of doom) a green beast with scales running across her back, with wings larger than buildings!

Barry flew up to sit on Melissa's neck, he swished his sword and she roared with all her might. Quickly, Johnny opened the bottle and collected the dragon's breath, before they knew it, they had sped past the dragon, and the malevolent maple towered over them. Suddenly, they all realised that this task would not be as easy as they thought it would be. The tree moved quickly to block them. Ralph sliced at the bark from the tree with his axe, the boys were about to hop on to Barry's back to escape, but they were too late, the tree swiped at Barry and he was stuck in its grip. Barry was caught; there was no way that he could escape. Barry told the others to run. It was a worthy sacrifice, but a great loss of a true friend.

Ralph and Johnny knew that they would cherish the moments they had together with Barry, and that he would always be in their hearts – forever. Returning to the wise wizard to create the potion. He used the speckled Nokiong berries, the rancid dragon's breath, and the bark of the malevolent maple. The potion was created, they poured it over the steering wheel and the taxi sped into the wall to get them back to Earth. They both made a solemn promise that they would never talk about this adventure ever again.

The Powerful Portal
by Silas Santell aged 11

On a cold dark night, all was quiet except the hooting birds and the howling wind, suddenly the air became warm, the street lit up with an enormous BANG! Then all was quiet again but there was one tiny taxi in the middle of the road.

It was a normal day and Jack was leaving his house to go to work, he worked at a mapping company that makes maps and figures out where everything is. Every morning that he goes to work he takes a taxi. But this was not the normal workday he was expecting.
When he got to work, he started plotting maps as usual.
Everything was normal until one peculiar person walked into the building, Jack noticed this and realized that this person was watching him.
He also saw the person's name tag, it said 'Xavier'.
When he finished work, he, as usual, called his taxi but when he got in the car, there was the stranger, Xavier.
Suddenly there was a big BANG! and it felt like they just teleported into a new world, and Jack could see they were flying.
Jack became nauseous and passed out!

Jack woke up and saw Xavier looking at him.
"Who are you?" asked Jack.
"I am Xavier as you probably know, I need you to come and help me," Xavier replied. Jack now was confused.
"Ok, but what do you want and why do you need me?" Jack said. "Also, where are we"
"What I want is to help the planets and realms and I need your mapping skills to locate and travel to different worlds and find different ingredients

that will make the Ever tree potion, then my magic taxi will help us deliver it."

"I don't know what this Ever tree potion is, and I don't exactly want to know."

"Too bad because you are going to know," replied Xavier, "on to the first world."

"Wait what are we doing?"

BANG! all of a sudden there was a big flash of light and then they were on a tiny island in the middle of the ocean.

"Where are we?" asked Jack, "and why did you bring me here?"

"We are in Oceadore, the water planet," replied Xavier, "and I bought you here because I need you."

"Ok, I get that but why do you need my mapping skills?" Jack asked.

"I need mapping skills to locate the ingredients and to figure out where we need to go," replied Xavier.

"But I don't want to help you, and this is a flooded planet. I can only figure out how deep it is."

Jack did some quick calculations and sometime later he had an answer, Xavier got some scuba gear from the car and then they set off under the deep dark blue blanket of water.

They swam for a while until they saw a beautiful big city filled with a bunch of colourful merpeople.

Then they saw… A GIGANTIC ugly Kraken!

They quickly got behind a rock because the Kraken noticed that they were invading its space.

Jack didn't know what to do he could see flying tentacles everywhere all of a sudden, the taxi car came through the water and gave them a big machine. Xavier used it and the Kraken screeched in pain and let out so much ink that they could not see. Xavier got a bottle and took some of the ink there was something weird about the ink it was glowing, and it made them feel dizzy. they got back in the car and then they sped up to the surface. When they reached the top, they took off their scuba gear and then talked about what they had just seen. Although Jack was still mad about being bought here, he was ready for the next adventure… BANG!

When they arrived, Xavier told Jack about the planet and how it was a forest with a maze in the middle. They had to get to the middle to kill a basilisk because their next ingredient was basilisk poison, they set off into the forest looking for the maze.
They both had a bright sword with a colour changing ruby in it which was the only thing that could kill a basilisk.
It took a long time to find the maze on the way they came across pixies and different magical creatures. They eventually found it because they followed a little fairy witch to the maze entrance.
When they reached the maze, Xavier realised he was so tall he could almost see above it. Jack thought of an idea, if they combined their heights they could see over the top. Xavier lifted Jack up, and they easily got to the middle.
There it was a giant, green, scaly snake that was sleeping so they thought they could easily kill it, but it woke up from its slumber. RUN!
Xavier, who was very brave, jumped over the beast and killed it; they took its fang, squirted its poison into a jar, and were off once again.

BANG! Again, they were off. Xavier did a ritual from a spell book and created a vibrant object. It looked really mesmerizing and was almost drawing Jack into the object.
Jack turned away from it and guided them to the next place they needed to go, it was in the middle of the galaxy.

There nothing was there apart from the deep, dark void and the taxi cab. Xavier got his spell book out again and went to the magic portal section, which held the key to getting home safely.

Jack, who was watching everything Xavier was doing, knew this was almost time to say goodbye.

Xavier put the strange object in the middle of the void and said some weird words and then all of a sudden, the void rippled, and then BOOM! And the portal was created.

"So, this is it? Goodbye?" asked Jack sadly.

Xavier replied, "It is never really goodbye. I will come and see you again. As they say in German… Auf Wiedersehen!"

The Cat Taxi Service
by Selina Brown aged 10

I put down my phone and looked into the mist in front of me, I could barely see anything but the dim light of a lamp post. Out of the gloom, I saw the taxi I ordered rapidly approaching me. The taxi suddenly appeared at my side and I nervously walked towards the driver's side. The taxi driver rolled down his window and I gasped…

The large cat looked at me suspiciously.

"Are you Willow?" it asked.

I nodded and rubbed my eyes in amazement. A cat was talking to me!

"Hop in then! We're off on a trip," the cat said.

I opened the door and placed myself down on one of the leather seats, I helped myself to one of the chocolate bars I found in a jar.

A part of me was burning with curiosity and I wanted to stay in the taxi with the cat whilst another part of me was frightened and screaming at me to escape.

I couldn't believe I was trusting a talking cat to drive a car!

Out the window, there was nobody in sight, a ghost town. The feline looked at me in the rear-view mirror.

"So! Where do you want to go? I can take you anywhere you desire…"

'Anywhere?' I thought to myself.

"I- I want to go to see a rainbow!" I said excitedly

"Off we go!" The cat squealed

The taxi jolted forwards and tilted onto its back wheels. I held onto the seat and squeezed my eyes shut.

"Look at the view! Don't be afraid!" the cat cried out.

I reluctantly peered out of the open window and saw shimmering gossamer wings, sprouting from the sides of the taxi!

The car lifted off into the air and a burst of wind blew into my face. We zoomed across the city, quicker than light. An iridescent rainbow shone brightly in the distance and after a few seconds, I was standing right in front of it. As I walked up to the rainbow and touched it, a burst of warmth and energy filled my bones. I smiled and looked back at the cat.

"What now?" he asked, grinning

"Let's climb it!" I exclaimed, planting my hand firmly onto the rainbow. We climbed the shimmering beam quicker than I expected. Every step I ascended made me feel happier than the last, and at the top, I was feeling elated. Beside me, the cat elegantly leaped up and up, his fur coat glinting in the sun.

At the top, I sat down and stared into the verdant green forests and blooming meadows below me. We stayed there until we saw the sunset. We slid down the other side of the rainbow, screaming in delight. When we reached the ground, a small creature hopped towards me. I looked closer and saw it was a leprechaun! It held out its hands and dropped an object into my hands. Don't look at it yet, the leprechaun's eyes seemed to say.

"So, where do you want to go next, eh?" the cat said.

"I think… now I want to go underwater in the ocean!" I exclaimed.

Thanking the leprechaun for its present, I settled back in the taxi. The cat drove it towards a sandy beach. Instead of having wings this time, the taxi transformed into a boat! The feline propped itself at the helm as I climbed up the rigging into the crow's nest. We started to go deeper into the depths of the water, safe under a strange bubble that surrounded the boat.

"Let's get out here, I think we are deep enough," I called to the cat.

I climbed down the net and jumped down onto the seabed. The water was clear, and shoals of fish swirled around us. I suddenly realised I needed to breathe if I wanted to survive. The cat stared at me calmly with his big amber eyes.

"Willow, I'm a magic cat. We can breathe and talk underwater," he explained.

I opened my mouth to reply in shock, but then immediately closed it. So many weird things had happened in the past couple of hours, so how strange was this really? The cat smiled at me and held out his paw. A mysterious shadow suddenly swept past me, making me spin round. 'What was that...?' I thought worriedly. More shadows appeared, surrounding us.

"What do you want? Come out and show us who you are!" I said timidly, my voice trembling in fear.

One by one, they came into the light. I gasped...

MERMAIDS?! I thought in amazement

"Are you a friend or foe?" one of the mermaids asked, glaring suspiciously at us.

"A friend! We won't hurt you," I said gently.

Muttering and chattering quickly spread around the group of mermaids. The smallest of the group stepped forward.

"Will you help us? Our Queen is terribly sick," she whispered.

"Of course! Lead us there!" I exclaimed.

We followed them into a huge sandcastle, decorated with colourful shells. They lead us into a room, where a pale mermaid, that had a shiny crown on her head, lay on a four-poster bed. She looked weak and feeble, as if she couldn't last much longer...

"We need a magical coin from a leprechaun. The only problem is that it's impossible as leprechauns are almost extinct," the smallest mermaid from earlier explained sadly.

I suddenly remembered that the leprechaun we saw at the rainbow gave me something! I reached into my pocket and brought out a golden coin, its light dazzled me.

"That's it! That's a legendary coin! Our Queen will be healed!" she cried in astonishment.

"Here," I said handing it to her. "You need it more than I do."

The tiny mermaid placed the gold coin onto the Mermaid Queen's forehead. A burst of light shone into her crown and she sat up and gasped.

"Thank you!" The Mermaid Queen exclaimed. "How can I ever repay you?!"

I looked at her necklace. "I like that! It's so pretty," I said, mesmerised

"Have it!" She laughed, "Think of it as a reward for healing me."

The cat nudged me gently.

"We have to get you back home," he said. The mermaids hugged us and waved goodbye as we swam back to the ship. As we rose back to the surface, it transformed back to the taxi and I fell fast asleep.

I woke up with a start. Wherever I was, it was dark. I squinted and could just make out the familiar shapes of my desk and wardrobe. Suddenly, my head started throbbing painfully. Sighing, I stretched out my arm and fumbled blindly in the direction of my bedside table, searching for the glass of water I always kept there. My hands knocked something cold and hard. Confused, I flicked on my lamp, wincing in the sudden brightness. Glinting in the light, lay a golden necklace. My mind started racing. Was it just an extremely vivid dream? That would make sense but what about the necklace? This whole thing was just too confusing. Suddenly, the necklace started vibrating in my hands. Was it calling me? I tentatively fastened it around my neck. Immediately, I was overcome with strange sensations. I could smell the sweet aroma of wildflowers, hear the gentle energised crackle of the rainbow, taste the strong salty air, feel the mermaids' glossy, flowing hair. But best of all, was the sound of the cat's smooth voice in my ear. It's been a long time since I went on my adventure with the cat and his magic taxi. Sometimes I ask myself whether I made it all up in my head. But then I just walk over to my dresser and gently take the golden necklace out of its glass display case. The cat's voice speaks into my ear and reminds me to keep believing in magic.

The Taxi to Impossible places
by Olivia Bunimovich aged 10

Two twins. One adventure. Can they keep it together?

One taxi, one day, one driver, two people. That was Autumn Blackstone's recipe for an adventure of a lifetime.

It was a typical winter morning for the Blackstone family.

Julia Blackstone and her kids, Autumn and Matteo, were getting ready for a typical day.

Hamen Blackstone, their dad, was already at work.

"Autumn!" Matteo shrieked. "We're going to be late for school if you don't pick up the pace!" Matteo Blackstone was Autumn's twin, and one of the most, wait no, the most popular kid in the whole of year 9 in the local school.

"I'm waiting for you!" Autumn Blackstone was the polar opposite of her brother. Unlike Matteo, Autumn was a quiet, caring figure, who never did anything without thinking about it first. Based on how shy she was Autumn's social status in school was not ideal. Julia blew a kiss to her children and hopped on her bike to go to work.

"I hate winter," Matteo complained.

"You hate summer too," Autumn stated.

She did not understand. How could someone find something bad in everything and yet seem so optimistic and chatty in school? Either he was an incredibly good actor, or she just wasn't getting something.

"Where on earth is this taxi!" Matteo tapped his foot on the pavement. After what seemed like forever, a shiny, black taxi pulled up to the curb.

"About time!" Classic Matteo. No filter whatsoever.

After apologising to the embarrassed taxi driver, Autumn hopped in, tossing her long, chestnut waves behind her. This was how it always was. Autumn felt she had to constantly clean up her brother's mess. Autumn kept on telling herself that it was her choice, that no-one was telling her to do it, but there was one major problem. Autumn cared. She cared about the taxi driver, she cared about the homeless people on the street, she even cared about her neighbour's second cousin (whom she never met). The whole drive she glanced out the window, thinking deep thoughts.

The pair finally arrived at school. The yard was empty.

"No, no. We're late. Late!" Matteo ranted.

"Being late was cool, last time I checked."

Matteo let out a loud, dismissive groan. "No, Autumn, that is so last season!" Autumn tended not to keep up with the trends, she could never understand the changes.

Still looking down at his phone, Matteo opened the door and got out, Autumn said, "thank you," to the driver and trailed behind.

"M-m-matteo?"

He didn't answer Autumn.

"W-where are we?"

At this, Matteo looked up. His eyes popped out of his head. They were no longer at school.

The siblings stood in an open area, filled with long, green grass. All around them were the tallest trees they had ever seen, even taller than the one in Trafalgar square at Christmas. January was Autumn's least favourite month of the year as the bitter cold would bite at her when she had to go to get the groceries, and she would have a sick feeling in her stomach when she saw the homeless people on the pavement, sick and freezing to their death. In January it was always cold and there was no Christmas to look forward to. But here it didn't seem to be winter.

"Did we somehow shoot to the northern hemisphere, Autumn?"

Geography was never Matteo's strong spot.

"Really? London is in the northern hemisphere!" Autumn secretly enjoyed correcting her brother.

There was a rustle in the bushes.

All of a sudden, a creature leaped out.

It was too much for Matteo to take. He dropped to the floor with a thud.

Autumn stared, wide-eyed, forgetting how to think, speak, or move.

The creature gave her the feeling of déjà vu. She had seen it before, but it was physically impossible. She couldn't have...

It seemed almost as terrified at the sight of Autumn as she was at the sight of it. Neither of them dared to say a word. The deafening silence continued for centuries until it said. "Who? What? Um...."

The creature looked like the average thirty-year-old man, with brown hair and a scraggly beard, but from the waist down he had the legs of a white stallion! His bony legs looked indestructible, and his swaying white tail was a bundle of silk.

Then it hit Autumn like a ton of bricks. She had seen him before! He looked exactly like a character from her favourite movie. And she knew this centaur's name was Charles.

"Uh, what? Who is this?" Matteo grunted, peeling his body off the ground.

After a long conversation, Charles explained things, but Matteo was really not getting it.

Matteo said, "Okay, so, we are in a land called Scar, you are a centaur and these rebels called The Other Side want to take over Scar, end the constitutional democracy, and set up a strict monarchy? Am I living in a fairy tale, because this sounds like an extract from one!"

The next things that happened were all a blur. A long metal rod smashed into the earth with a thundering clamour, then exploded like a bomb, sending Autumn flying back, a deafening sound ringing in her ears.

Two weeks later, she woke up, wrapped in a giant leaf. A cast stiffly sat around her leg, pain scorching her.

"Autumn, I'm so sorry. Your brother didn't make it. I... I just..." And unsure what else to say, Charles bounded out of the room.

Too sad to cry, too shocked to scream, Autumn just lay there. Her brother, <u>her</u> family member, her twin! He couldn't be gone. It was too tragic to be true. Matteo was half of her, and she just could not live with only half of herself.

Finally, the tears and screams came. She would never leave Scar! She would never show her face again!

Her eyes glistening, her throat hoarse, she limped out of the medical centre. There, in the middle of the forest, was the taxi cab. Without thinking, she ran to it, forgetting her leg, and flung the door open, she sat down and buried her head in her arms. The taxi halted to a stop, and Autumn looked up....

To find Matteo sitting there on the curb, looking at his phone.

"Matteo!?!?" She screamed. Without a second thought, she threw herself at him and hugged him fiercely. There was no sign of him knowing what had happened.

"Auty, are you okay?" he warily asked. Forcing herself to let him go, she replied with a glow in her eyes, "Never been better."

Felicity
by Joss Steel aged 12

I'm nervous, no, I'm terrified; it's that kind of fear that sits in the very bottom of your stomach and refuses to leave no matter how much distraction or consolation you receive. It's the kind of fear that makes you want to be sick and cry at the same time – the kind of fear that you know you would do anything to get rid of.

"Felicity!" A voice shouts. This is my mum. She is the best mum you could wish for. She is clever without being egotistical, slightly immature, but not annoyingly so, and is always, always kind. She has constantly been there for me, I don't know why though, as I think I am more of an inconvenience than a reward.

"We're nearly there, are you ok?"

"I'm fine," I reply. Fine is an interesting word, as it very rarely means what it is meant to mean. You could say you are fine and mean you are really fine but in this case, as in most cases, it means I am really not fine but don't want to talk about it. By the way, I'm Felicity – I'm thirteen and have been in a wheelchair all of my life. I'm relatively smart and play basketball. Apparently, my name derived from the Greek word for happiness yet there hasn't been much of that in my life. Today I am going to find out if I am having another operation, as the last thirteen haven't worked. Fourteenth time lucky?

The thing about me and regular travel is we have a slight disagreement with each other, well a major one to be honest. After the half an hour journey for me that would be a 2-minute walk for others, we are just about to leave Paddington station. People say that after you've done something many times it becomes less daunting – people lie.

My mum is trying to flag down a black cab when the brake on my wheelchair unlocks. The next thing I know I'm rolling away, picking up speed, soaring like a rocket, hurling towards the worst place to be, the road. I'm screaming, but at that moment I am powerless, I don't know what to do. As I move towards the road, an ominous, black shape approaches, a black cab, will that be my destiny? I collide with the cab, my mind whirling with my almost inevitable fate. I try to move but I don't feel anything. I miss my mother's warm touch. I miss everything.

After contemplating my options, I decide to accept my fate, it's easier that way, right? Although, all I can think about is that black shape with its smooth, shiny edges and its orange sign holding four, now deadly, letters. T A X I.

I wake up in a bed surrounded by a jungle of machinery and wires. My mum is sitting next to me and jumps at the sight of me with my eyes open, as if she had forgotten I was there.

"Are you ok?"

"I'm fine," I reply, and I really was fine.

The next thing I know she is pulling down the covers and unhooking all the machines attached to me. Then, to my utter confusion, she gestures at me to stand up. Hesitantly, I roll over and to my sheer glee, my legs move with me as if they didn't have a mind of their own. Even more hesitantly I attempt to stand, although not with much hope that I would be successful, and I am able to. I almost fall over with the shock. I can stand! Me! I can stand!

With no more thought, I run out of the room and out of the hospital. For the first time in my life, I am experiencing things that so many people take for granted. I run into the park, only then realising that I'm not wearing shoes, and not caring in the slightest. I feel the rich soil under my feet, sucking in every texture, every bump, every scrape. There is a swing in the park which I bolt for – another thing I have never been able to experience properly. Weirdly, I hear the faint sound of a siren in the back of my head, but the buzzing of my excitement blocks it out. As I start to swing, I feel the cold, autumn air brush against my cheek, the joyous feeling at the bottom of my stomach, and happiness clouds my brain.

Out of the corner of my eye, I spot a river, I run, feeling invincible, and jump into it (fully clothed). The coldness of the river doesn't bother me. I feel the marvellous sensation of the water slapping my feet and the quietness of the world when I dive below. It's interesting how centimetres of difference can create complete serenity.

"She's crashing," I hear a voice. Suddenly, I'm falling, but not through the water – through nothingness. It is swallowing me, darkness clouding my brain.

I'm five, it's my birthday and I am going downstairs - my mum is helping me. I see a pile of presents taller than me stacked up on the table. There are spectacular decorations coating the room in every colour you can think of. There is a beautiful cake badly hidden in the corner. The table has lots of little bowls containing all of my favourite things - the room is filled with joy. I look around at everything and want it to last forever, I want this moment to last forever.

My head merges into reality – again I am in a hospital bed surrounded by a jungle of wires, but this time I have a horrible feeling pulsing in my head, and every part of my body aches. My mum is sitting near me, her hand firmly gripping my arm, it hurts a little, but I don't care. It is my mum – she is holding me. Also, in my room is a cavalry of doctors – why? I do not know.

"Are you ok?" my mum asks

"I'm fine" I reply

I was not fine.

I flexed my toes in frustration. Wait!

Taxi Cab 54321
by Verity Callaghan aged 9

Katie is an ordinary 10-year-old, she lives with an ordinary family and she has a life in an ordinary world or at least she thought she did.

Today Katie was really excited because she was travelling to the airport to fly to Spain on holiday. Her suitcase was all packed with her favourite clothes and dresses. Her little brother George is so obsessed with rockets he's packed 2 whole suitcases with rockets only!

The taxi cab arrived and they all ran out of the house with joy, but then they all stopped in disappointment as they looked at the cab.

"Eww, it's mouldy," groaned Katie.

"It looks like it won't even get to the end of the road," said Mum.

"I guess we'll have to get in."

Dad started lifting all the heavy suitcases into the rusty boot.

"Come on give me your rocket," said Dad.

"No!" said George, "I'm going to play with it in the taxi."

"Ok," replied Dad, "get in then."

So, they all took their seats in the cab.

"Look they are half ripped apart," said George.

"And it smells like stale cheese sandwiches," said Katie.

The taxi driver was dressed surprisingly smart and began trying to start the cab, he tried so many times that Dad started yawning and feeling sleepy.

Mum rolled her eyes, "we'll never get to the end of the road," she moaned again.

"5-4-3-2-1 BLAST OFF!" shouted George.

"Sshhh!" said Mum.

Just as she was saying that a loud creaking scratching sound started, and a deep dark hole suddenly opened up in the bottom of the cab.

"What is that"? asked Katie.

"I don't know," replied Dad with a puzzled look on his face.

"Can I go in and take a look"? asked Katie.

"Yeah, yeah I want to go in too!" shouted George.

"Be quiet please," said Mum.

"Go on then but be careful," said Dad.

"I promise we will back a few minutes," replied Katie.

So, both of them jumped in at the same time.

"Ahhhhhhhhhhhhhh!!" They shouted as they magically disappeared.

"Hello, hello?" called Mum and Dad.

"Where have they gone?" Mum said with a worried tone in her voice.

"They'll be back any time soon," said the cab driver with a smile.

With a big bang, both children hit the ground with a thump.

"Where are we?" said George.

"I really don't know," answered Katie.

"Look there's a candy house," said George excitedly as he started running towards it.

"Yum, yum, yum, oohh strawberry laces my favourite!"

There were pear drops, sherbet lemons, liquorice of every colour of the rainbow, lollipops, cola sours and jelly sweets.

"Wow!" said Katie, "that sherbet lemon is delicious."

"I could stay here for years," shouted George stuffing his mouth full of candy.

In less than two minutes they both fell to the ground, so full of sugar that they could barely walk.

"We need to go before we have a major sugar rush," moaned Katie.

They both started slowly walking, both groaning because they had eaten too much.

It felt as if they had been walking for about an hour and they were getting really bored, suddenly the temperature began to fall. It was freezing cold and their teeth started chattering.
"Wwwhy is iiit ssso cccold"? Asked George his teeth rattling together.
"I ddon'tt kknow," replied Katie, "bbutt look eeeverything is ice creammm."
George ran over to a lamp post and hesitantly licked it, "mmm this tastes like salted caramel," he said.
"Ooohh, this bark of a tree tastes like triple chocolate!" said Katie.
"This car is defiantly raspberry ripple," George said whist he was licking the wing mirror.
"And the wheel of this car is mint choc chip," said Katie.
"I'm getting bad brain freeze," said George holding his head.
"Ow my mouth is freezing cold and it hurts," said Katie holding her tongue out.
So, both of them started walking away, both moaning and groaning about the pain.

After a while, they went quiet and concentrated on walking, but then George spotted a field of flowers. Looking closer he noticed that it wasn't a normal field of flowers but a field of donut flowers swaying in the breeze.
"Wow look," said Katie, "there is a paddling pool full of donuts!"
"My favourite is chocolate iced donuts," shouted George.
"Mine is jammy ones," said Katie excitedly.
"Look," said George, "there is a donut in the shape of a rocket."
He picked it up and started playing with it, swooping it through the air, "5-4-3-2-1 BLAST OFF!!!!" Suddenly everything went blank the donuts disappeared, as quick as a flash they were sitting back in the taxi.

"You're back," said a familiar voice, it was Dad! "
Good children," said Mum, "you promised us you would be back in a couple of minutes and you were."

Katie and George sat there confused, they thought they had been away for hours.

"Wait I'm confused." Said Katie turning to George with a puzzled look on her face.

The taxi driver started the engine with a single turn of the key, and they set off for the airport. "We're finally on our way," said Dad, as Mum rustled in her handbag and pulled out a round metal tin.

"Anyone for a cherry travel sweetie?" asked Mum.

"Oh no, not more sugar!" cried Katie and George together.

The Video Game Adventure
by Ruairidh H aged 10

One very odd night I woke up in the early hours, it was still dark, feeling like I hadn't had any sleep in days. I tossed and turned but couldn't get back to sleep, so I got up and put my clothes on and went downstairs as quick as a superhero, because I realised, I was very hungry. I got some food and as I was about to grab a drink, I noticed there was a very bright light from outside shining through the curtains. I didn't know what was outside because the curtains were closed.

I was very confused, and I didn't know what to do, when all of a sudden, the very bright light was gone. I opened the door and there was a taxi outside. I was curious so I grabbed my bag and food and went out and looked inside the taxi window. I realised there was no driver. I opened the door and got in to investigate, but the door slammed behind me and the taxi started to move. I was getting a little freaked out and tried to open the door, but it was locked. I unlocked it but it locked itself again, I kept trying but the same thing just kept happening. After a while (it felt like hours) the taxi stopped, the door opened, and the seat catapulted me out. I stood up and in front of me was a creepy old house. I was rather freaked out and just a little bit scared.

The bright light suddenly came back and then the taxi was gone.

I hardly had time to think before I was teleported into the house.

I was standing in a dark hallway when suddenly five blue fairies were circling me, and they all had black sparkling wands. They were waving their wands and saying spells, the house started to swirl, and I had to close my eyes as I was getting dizzy. When I opened my eyes, I was astounded as the house looked like a house out of a video game.

The fairies said, "Ruairidh, welcome to the wooded mansion in your own video game. You are now a character in the game, and you need to complete four tasks to get back to your own bed in your own house. But there are consequences if you fail.

You will be given tools in a special bag to complete these tasks which are on 4 different levels.

The tasks are

1. Find a diamond in the Sea of Jewels.
2. Find and eat a Lapus apple in the orchard of delicious fruits.
3. Rescue the golden parrot from the golden treehouse.
4. Get back to Wooded Mansion.

There are rules that you need to know about

1. You have only three lives.
2. No-one can help you.
3. If you skip a level, there are consequences, and you need to make choices. If you skip a level you either have to throw away two of your tools, lose a life, or you have to throw away all of your tools but you can have an extra life. It is your choice, so choose wisely as some are better than others but you will never know.
4. You must complete all of this in ONE week or you will FAIL

Your time starts in ten seconds so be prepared for the adventures ahead of you. Goodbye Ruairidh."

Before I could say anything, the ten seconds passed, and the game started and then everything went swirly again

I opened my eyes, and I was standing on a platform staring down at a massive ocean full of jewels, but I couldn't see a diamond anywhere. I looked in the tool bag I was given by the fairies and saw a tiny raft. As soon as I pulled it out it went, 'poof', and became a huge raft.

I jumped on it and started to sail around. After 2 hours out of the corner of my eye, I saw the diamond. But as I was about to grab it a massive tidal wave appeared in the distance. I reached in as quickly as I could to grab the diamond, but it sank to the bottom. I quickly checked the bag and found a scuba diving kit. I put it on and dived to the bottom and grabbed the diamond. As a grabbed it things went swirly again.

When I opened my eyes, I was in an orchard full of lots of ordinary apples. I couldn't see a Lapus apple anywhere and they are easy to find because they are blue. I searched for days and couldn't find one and was running out of time so decided I needed to skip a level. Now I only had two lives left. Again, it went swirly.

When I opened my eyes there was writing in front of me. It said you have one day left. When I read it, I was shocked that I had used so much time. In front of me was another bag but when I went to grab it, I noticed my tool bag was gone. I looked in the new bag and there were 3 new tools. There was a titanium axe, a birdcage, and a compass. I remembered that one of the fairies was holding a sign that said 'South'. It confused me at first but now I understood why she had that. I used the compass and started heading south and came across the golden treehouse after a few hours of walking.

I found the golden parrots lair, but the only problem was it was at the top of the tallest tree in the forest. I looked in my tool bag and remembered I had the titanium axe. I chopped down the tree and grabbed the parrot and put him in the birdcage.

Everything went swirly.

I was on the final level and the writing popped up to say I had 5 minutes to finish and it also said underneath that all I could use to complete the game was the things I had collected. I pulled out the diamond and the parrot tried to get out of the cage to grab it. I let the parrot out and gave him the diamond. He swallowed it and transformed into a golden dragon. I jumped on his back and we flew to the Wooded Mansion, we arrived with a millisecond left.

The fairies were there and said.

"Congratulations Ruairidh, you finished the game. You are a Champion!"

And the swirly thing happened again. I was back home on the sofa like nothing had happened.

The Magical Keys
by Isaac Manuell aged 8

One morning it was Ben's birthday.

He got £40! He didn't normally get £40, but his stepdad gave it to him the night before, after coming home late and smelling of beer.

He decided to spend his money by going to school in a taxi cab.

He called for the cab and waited outside.

A portal appeared in the street, it looked like a circular rainbow.

A taxi cab came through it. The taxi was dark as coal. He opened the taxi cab door and got in. The driver looked strange with long grey hair over his deeply wrinkled skin.

He wore a black cloak as dark as night.

The driver's tired face was as pale as the moon.

He asked where Ben wanted to go. Ben said he wanted to go to his school. The driver asked him for £10 and shouted, "Abracadabra!"

A portal opened in front of the taxi. They drove through and found themselves in front of St Glen's Primary school.

Ben left the taxi and skipped merrily into the school playground. He spent his whole day thinking about his funny morning journey to school. It was better than taking three buses full of miserable dull faces. After school, Ben went to the nearest telephone box. He called the taxi cab again. Just like before, a rippling portal opened and the taxi cab came through it.

Ben got in and paid the old mystical driver his money and found himself in front of his tall flats again.

Ben's mother asked him how he got home so quickly.

Ben said he had called a taxi cab on his own and his mother frowned.

The next day Ben called for the taxi cab again.

This time it took longer than before for it to arrive and no portal opened. As Ben got in, he could see that the driver looked miserable and glum.

"What's the matter?" Ben asked.

"My brother stole my precious magic keys," replied the driver.

"Your brother?" Ben questioned. "Why did he do that?"

"He's been really jealous ever since father gave the amazing magic keys to me and not to him."

"Why didn't your dad give your brother the keys?" Ben asked curiously.

"He didn't trust him." The driver continued, "these magical keys make me able to travel through time and space, and our father knew that Aaron, my brother, couldn't be trusted with them. Last night, Aaron came into my house and stole the one key that allows me to travel through space."

"What about the time key?" Ben blurted.

"I still have that. Otherwise, I would have been even later in arriving here." the driver said.

"Why don't you use the time key to travel back in time and catch your brother before he steals the space key?" Ben said with a smile.

"Of course!" The driver cried loudly, his miserable face coming to life again. He muttered a spell and then the taxi cab was in front of a tall old house in the evening. They crept silently into the house and up the stairs. The driver saw his wicked brother sneaking quietly into his room. The driver leapt at him. Using a thick rope, the driver tied up Aaron and dragged him outside in the cold night air, while Ben called the police. The driver then took Ben back to Ben's school, at the correct time, and gave the power of flight to Ben for helping him.

Ben never had to take a bus again.

THE END.

C.A.A.B PUBLISHING

www.caabpublishing.co.uk

Visit our website www.caabpublishing,co.uk to keep up to date with our future competitions as well as to find other books by our amazing authors.

Some of our books for younger readers:

The Gem Masters Series – Join Lara as she travels to the Land of the Gem Masters to find her mother and fulfil her destiny.

Twisty Tales – Fabulously twisted tales for children from F.J. Beerling & V.A. Bryce.

The Wishing Well Collection – Travel to the fairy kingdom of Enchandream Wood and meet the Queen of the Fairies and her five magical daughters.